Stockton & Billingham College
T022087

D1098241

4339501003098442772612

HIT RECORD

HOW TO GET A HIT RECORD

Things You Should Know About The Pop Music Business

Ray Hammond

JAVELIN BOOKS
POOLE · DORSET

First published in the UK 1985 by Javelin Books,
Link House, West Street, Poole, Dorset, BH15 1LL

Distributed in the United States by
Sterling Publishing Co., Inc.,
2 Park Avenue, New York, NY 10016

British Library Cataloguing in Publication Data

Hammond, Ray
How to get a hit record : things you should know about the pop music business.
1. Music, Popular (Songs, etc.)—Vocational guidance
I. Title
780'.42'023 ML3470

ISBN 0 7137 1498 0

Typeset by Aquarius Typesetting Services,
New Milton, Hants.

Printed in Great Britain by
Hazell Watson & Viney Limited,
Member of the BPCC Group,
Aylesbury, Bucks.

CONTENTS

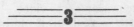

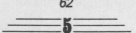

INTRODUCTION

In January 1972 the producer of a prestigious television rock programme leaned across my desk in my London office and told me that it would cost me £250 for my group to become the studio guests on his show. 'In cash, of course'. It was my first direct experience of 'payola', or corruption in the record business.

It was late, and only he and I were left in the office building I then rented for my management and production company in Marylebone High Street. This meeting was the climax of three weeks of work during which time I had courted the young producer and chauffeured him to three gigs in various parts of the UK to see the band I wanted him to book. The band had a new album released, were outstandingly good on stage and were 'right' for his show. Exposure on that show at that time would have got the album into the lower end of the album charts and would have ensured middle-bill bookings during the forthcoming summer festival season (very big in those 'heavy' days).

His demand for a bribe shattered the few illusions I had left about the pop business, or 'rock industry' as we then chose to call it. I had been a producer and manager for four years and, like everyone in the business, I had heard about payola, and hype, about managers who sent teams around the country buying up their artists' records, but I hadn't come face to face with it before.

Payola started in the 1950s in the USA when the pop music business was an infant. Alan Freed, the man who first coined the phrase 'rock 'n roll', admitted taking bribes to showcase certain new performers. He was tried and convicted in a public show trial designed to show the American public that the business had been cleaned up. Dick Clark, the host of the nation's first coast-to-coast rock 'n roll TV show was found to own the record company releasing the hit title he promoted. The age of innocence was over.

In Britain persistent reports of corruption were laid at the door of the business during the 1960s but with the exception of a few minor characters who were sacked for accepting favours under suspicious circumstances, there was no major UK uncovering of the fix until eighteen months after my encounter with the BBC producer who asked me for £250.

I did not have £250 that evening or the course of my life would undoubtedly have been different — not necessarily for the better, I suspect. I was in the process of going broke and £250 (the equivalent of £1,500 in the mid-1980s) could not be squeezed from my overdraft. The bribe was not paid and the band did not appear on that TV show. Their album didn't make the charts either.

The fatal connection for this producer, and for others like him, was made by that nationally-famous hypocritical champion of the people, *the News of the World.* A handful of hacks from the Street of Shame decided it would be a great story if they could bribe BBC producers to book no-hope acts. In the worst tradition of that and other newspapers they set themselves up as *agent provocateurs*, posing as managers of artists. They agreed to pay the fee demanded by the same producer who had previously propositioned me and they watched with glee as the appalling, talentless band they had selected to assist them in their execution appeared on national TV. After they published their experiences in the paper, that producer and several BBC radio producers were immediately sacked.

These revelations were followed up by many more and during 1973 the British music business was put under a magnifying glass as Scotland Yard delegated twenty detectives to interview 1,000 people. The investigations resulted in a 500 page document to the Director of Public Prosecutions and nine people were arrested and charged with corruption.

I quote this piece of history not to point out how corrupt the British music business was in the 1970s, but to point out how *innocent* it all was. The criminal activity was all directed at influencing the taste of the British public. The business as a whole recognized that in the end it was the people who decided what they liked and which records they bought. The aim of the corruption then was to find criminal ways of exposing their product to the public in order for the public to judge it.

Today most overt corruption has gone. DJs aren't paid cash to play records (although there is still a form of currency which often changes hands) and TV producers wouldn't receive a bribe even if they asked for one: quite the opposite. They're more likely to consider doing favours for the business in order to get an exclusive chance to show a group's new video. The shoe is on the other foot with a vengeance.

The UK music business now *controls* public taste: it doesn't seek to influence it, or manipulate it, it owns it. In recent years, there has been a fundamental change; the business is now so corrupt that, if viewed morally (as against legally), it makes the activities of those bribe-taking producers of the fifties, sixties and seventies look like kindergarten stuff.

In relative terms, the American music business remains 'pure'. It is still a business of hype, payola, scandal, fraud and talent simply because the market is far too large and diverse to be controlled in the way that I now consider the British music business to be controlled. Under normal circumstances the UK market for records would be far too small to attract the sophisticated and massive corruption which now has it under control: that sort of mighty money-making talent would be off and away working in other industries, were it not for the fact that the British hit-making factories are the *key to the world market*.

Manipulating the charts in Britain allows the men who own the business to make heavy money on the *international* market for a relatively small UK investment. Music that is successful in the British charts currently has a value far beyond local record sales. British chart success virtually guarantees chart success in the USA, Canada, Australia, the massive markets of South America and many other foreign language markets.

The manipulation of British adolescents is not the ultimate aim of the operation: the aim is to use Britain as a springboard to offshore money, to cheat the British tax system out of the results of such international success and to dominate the world's music business.

This scenario now occurs regularly. It may not sustain itself for many years — there has always been a yo-yo effect in the origination of trends between the USA and the UK — but it is far-reaching in its scope and money earning power. Several unique circumstances have combined to make this control possible: the complete control of public taste and the sustaining of artists with no real talent for long strings of hits.

Judge the effectiveness of the UK control: in 1983 British music captured 35 per cent of the best-selling singles and albums in the USA. Compare this to the peak penetration of British music in America in the Beatle-way of the mid-1960s: then British artists managed to capture only 20 per cent of the best-selling records and that was hailed as the 'British invasion' which eclipsed American talent. British records now have nearly twice the share of the American market they did twenty years ago.

The record business is now a mature, slow-growth industry which will never again see the massive explosion of profits witnessed in the 1960s. But if the market is now more predictable, more controllable, it is also much, much more profitable for individual acts and their managers or lawyers. Record companies, managers and producers can now extract much more profit from individual successful acts (in percentage terms) than they could twenty years ago. However, the artist's lot remains relatively unchanged.

To explain why British managers and record companies are prepared to hype UK acts to apparently 'uneconomic' levels, it is important to see the success of a world class act in global financial terms. The world-wide record business is worth $12,000,000,000. According to the BPI — the British Phonographic Industry Association — overseas royalties earned by British groups during 1983 totalled £300,000,000, a significant proportion of the world-wide total, and a sum larger than the industry's total sales of singles and albums and tapes in the UK in the same year.

So, if an act makes it big in Britain, it stands a fair chance of locking into this world-wide bonanza. The British pop business is easy to manipulate because it is so small, but its influence in the world market is out of all proportion to its size. It is as though one small state in the USA was producing 35 per cent of all national hits, 50 per cent of all European hits, 18 per cent of Japanese hits and 23.5 per cent of hits in the rest of the world.

Britain has become a hit factory.

THE NEW CORRUPTION

Corruption in the old days was easily definable; in the sense that a producer would have taken £250 to showcase an act on national TV, that offer was corrupt. But for 'corruption' you must now substitute a new word: 'marketing'. The UK business is dominated and run by marketing men (very, very few women) and new euphemisms have emerged to describe 'hyped' records.

A record which is destined for the Top 5 even before release is described as having 'priority'. This tag word ensures that every resource of the record company, producer, management office, video team, producers, clothes designers, publicists, record pluggers and advertising agents will be placed behind a single. How the business gets a priority single into the charts today is fundamentally more corrupt than trying to bribe a few unscrupulous DJs and producers. The fraud involves massive amounts of money and any performer who wants to join the elite, to become a star, needs to know how it is done.

1

You have talent. You can do something: sing, play an instrument, compose music or write lyrics. You might be a superb on-stage performer with a personality that launches itself through the lights to an audience. Whatever it is, you have to have something to offer if you want to make it in the pop music business.

Even very small and minor talents are eligible for pop success, however, and the business has a long history of such talents which have become successful by sheer application, by the ability to make the most out of very little. The problem you have on your road to superstardom is that the British music business has become *totally corrupt.*

Public taste is now manipulated by cynical marketing men who make the antics of the sixties and seventies hype merchants look pale by comparison.

HOW IT USED TO BE

Brian Epstein personally bought the Beatles' first single, *Love Me Do*, into the charts. The group had been signed by EMI partly because their manager owned a chain of record shops; it was good business sense to keep him sweet by spending a few hundred pounds recording a bunch of scruffs, one or more of whom he was hoping to sleep with.

EMI had no plans for the Beatles to become a smash success. Their marketing force was behind the clones of successful American artists: Cliff Richard and the Shadows, Adam Faith and Helen Shapiro. *Love Me Do* was never intended to do anything and when Epstein discovered that there was no advertising, no plugging and no promotion for the record he went back to Liverpool and ordered 10,000 copies of the record for his own NEMS shops. That sales figure alone should have been sufficient to put *Love Me Do* into the charts, as they were organised in those days. It didn't.

Epstein then arranged for every Beatles fan and every relative who could be contacted to embark on a letter-writing blitz to the BBC and Radio Luxembourg — then the only commercial radio station broadcasting across Britain. These 'arranged' letters flooded into the request shows and Epstein's helpers toured shops ordering and buying copies of *Love Me Do*, forcing bewildered record shop owners to search through the catalogues for the obscure release.

EMI were forced to make a second pressing of the record — they had only pressed a few more than Epstein's original 10,000 order — and then the company decided to swing behind the record to see what could be done. Within a week it was on the play list of the BBC Light Programme — (the forerunner of Radio 1) and the nation started to hear the songs and the sound of the Beatles.

Love Me Do slipped into the charts at 49 and staggered up to Number 17 before peaking, held back by the lack of launch advertising and trade awareness. George Martin rushed the group back into EMI's Abbey Road recording studios and recorded *Please Please Me* in a day.

This time EMI planned that the record should be a hit and provided the necessary promotion and exposure. It got to Number 2 and the Beatles were launched.

The reason for the history lesson is to illustrate several points: Lennon and McCartney are now generally regarded as the most talented songwriters ever produced by the modern pop industry. Certainly the Beatles were the most successful entertainment act of all time and, for those who don't remember it, held an importance in public life so great that it rivalled the public position of a President, Prime Minister or major film star. By comparison, Boy George, Michael Jackson, Frankie or even the Police have failed to make it. But unless Epstein had hyped the Beatles' first record it is doubtful whether the world would ever have heard any Lennon/McCartney songs. The methods he used were crude and today they would fail, but the lesson is clear: talent on its own is not enough.

For 25 years the British pop music industry and the charts around which it all revolves were a mixture of hype and talent. Those who did the hyping always maintained that only the performers with talent were worth hyping since they were the only ones who could sustain success. 'What is the point of hyping talentless performers?' they asked. 'They'll just be One Hit Wonders'.

There were, of course, many One Hit Wonders in the 1960s and some in the 1970s, but you will notice that they have almost disappeared in the eighties. I think that the One Hit Wonder act is now too expensive. It now costs about £500,000 to turn a record by a new act into a Top 5 hit, and takes three Top 3 records and two internationally successful albums to recover this kind of investment.

THE CHANGE IN THE BRITISH BUSINESS

From the mid-1950s up until 1980 the British music industry was made up of hype, talent, luck and questionable business methods. The people attracted to the management side of the business ranged from city accountants to convicted criminals, with the poorly-educated entrepreneural barrow-boy as the typical model. It was a hit and miss business with much fun, many threats, a little violence, a lot of drugs, a fair amount of glamour and, finally, some chance for those with talent to make it.

But this is no longer true of the British music business. You will still find the colourful managers, those who will seriously threaten to break your bones if you step out of line, but these showbiz 'characters' are on the way out. No one should mourn the passing of the few who actually did break bones — there were only two or three British managers who ever went in for such things — but the individual seat-of-the-pants manager and manipulator is disappearing. There are a few old timers desperately trying to make their old methods of hyping work in the new climate of computer-analysed and created charts, but their attempts fail pathetically and, one by one, they are going bankrupt or quitting the business.

In their place are highly-trained corporate executives, lawyers and accountants who, with network computing power, build 'models' of how the money will flow during a particular act's year and can create 'chart simulations' of sales through the most important record shops to ensure that their 'target marketing' (another new phrase for hype) fits neatly with the perceived performance of charting records. Gone is even the faintest chance for talent to make it on its own merit.

All through the period when managers like Epstein were hyping their artists into the charts, hits were happening for performers who weren't hyped — the 'genuine' hit which seemed to occur spontaneously and which reflected the real taste of the public. When viewed carefully, with the gift of hindsight, many of these 'natural' hits turn out, of course, to have been far less spontaneous than the circumstances suggested at the time. Some reflected the hard work artists had put in on tours, so that ready-made markets existed for the record. Other hits were made by individual, influential disc jockeys who decided to exercise their personal power to see what they could achieve. A few artists and songwriters really did catch the mood of a moment and reflect what ordinary kids felt.

Today almost every new act which enters the British Top 50 arrives there through activities which most record buyers would consider corrupt if they were made aware of the extent to which the market is manipulated. The word corruption needs to be defined in this context: it does not mean that DJs are paid money to play certain records. The days of direct 'Payola' are long gone, but payment is still made to DJs and producers on a regular basis. Only the currency has changed; it is now cocaine.

Neither does corruption mean that managers tour the country buying their own artists' records from dealers' shops (the chart returns are carefully watched by a sophisticated computer program to spot any 'suspect' sales — they are now manipulated much more effectively) and it doesn't mean that the charts themselves, now operated for the BBC by the Gallup organization, are 'fixed' in some overtly corrupt way. Gallup, and its associates in the compilation of the charts, are above reproach and struggle to keep the chart as representative as possible of public record-buying patterns.

What has been 'fixed' is far more subtle, and that is the record buyer. We are all now 'fixed' by careful marketing strategy, but just in case you think that this is no different from every other sort of 'fix' for products which are marketed using modern techniques, you should also know that the distribution system is also 'fixed' to limit the records available to you in your local record store and to bribe the record shop owners. This is now the sharp end of corruption in the music business.

BRIBERY IN THE OLD SENSE

'You take 40 of these new singles and I'll give you a box of twenty albums by XYZ'. This suggestion is usually made by a sales rep or van driver working for one of the major standard record distributors; it is the sort of deal struck over the counter of the nation's record shops every day. For 'XYZ' read any international top name.

The law of libel prevents those names being printed here, but the principle is simple: the record company salesman wants the dealer to buy 40 copies of a single by a new 'priority' band. To induce the dealer to do so, the rep gives the dealer twenty albums by a top-selling act which the dealer knows he can sell quickly at full price. The retail price of a typical album by a top-name act is around £6 and normally the dealer has to pay £3.50 for each copy, making £2.50 profit per record sold. If a dealer receives twenty albums by a top name (free of charge), the profit is obviously the full £120. But there is more to it than that: the record company frequently arranges to supply the records free of paperwork as well, so that the transaction never appears on the accounts, either the record company's or the record dealer's. If this happens, the dealer's £6 per record is worth a lot more to him than the same sum if it were then going to have to go through his books and be subject to tax. And, if by a rare mischance the 40 'priority' singles he bought should stick, he could write them off against any other profit he is forced to declare.

Thus in a single move, the dealer takes cash for his back pocket and has gained himself the chance to make more profit for the 40 singles he buys legitimately or, at the worst, helped to keep down the declared profit while increasing his personal cash take out of the business, this is a trick that many entrepreneural people might want to achieve in our highly-taxed society. Those whose job it is to try and keep the charts representative have long been aware of this threat to straight dealing in the record shops.

HIT TIP

It is important to stress that the Gallup organization, which compiles the Charts, is aware of 'extra-ordinary marketing support' when it occurs and 'weights' a record's chart placing according to the amount of marketing involved. This is, of course, a subjective operation which cannot alter the fact that highly-promoted records are stocked in preference to those without such support, limiting the public's choice. The end result is that chart positions are being adjusted between records which are all receiving priority treatment. Those without such support don't show at all.

Gallup has laid down a special 'code of conduct' which limits the type of free gifts which may be given away as 'promotional items' such as badges, buttons and patches — or a free record *by the same artist* — shall be provided free to dealers. However, during research for this book, I have been told repeatedly that this code is ignored by sales and promotion staff from almost every major wholesaler and I have personal experience of the hypocrisy of the 'leaders' of the industry. Managing directors and chairmen of record companies are frequently launching public attacks on the 'freebie racket' and other non-acceptable promotional activities while at the same time personally instructing their sales force to break the Gallup chart code.

Gallup insists that the majority of the 255 shops which contribute their sales returns to make up the charts (backed up by a further 400 shops which form a cross-check panel) do not help record companies manipulate the charts, but my research suggests that the practice of 'dealer stroking' by record company representatives is endemic and considered the norm by most record shops lucky enough to be on the chart compilation list.

Record shops are now paying £1,000 to buy the computer terminals which allow them to contribute returns to Gallup's chart computers. In the light of the fact that record shops don't get paid for the extra work of keying in sales returns to the Dataports, it must be asked why these shopkeepers are so keen to spend their money to help Gallup compile the charts. The reason is that becoming a 'chart shop' is the difference between merely making a living and making a fortune.

Gallup explains this phenomenon by suggesting that dealers get better treatment from record companies when they contribute their sales figures to the charts. Gallup carried out a lengthy survey in 1983 which revealed that shops with Dataports which contributed chart information get better terms from record companies, which allowed them to sell their records at lower prices than non-chart shops. It also showed that chart dealers were always the ones to get 12-inch 'special' singles, picture discs, records in special sleeves and record company promotional material.

This is only the surface manifestation of what occurs, however. Britain is such a small territory when compared to the USA that it is easy for a large record company or record distributor to pay close attention to 250 record shops (and to the 400 back-up shops). In order to get a hit, the record company only has to make sure the record is selling through these outlets to gain a lower-end chart placing. After that, air play and TV exposure pick up and, if the record is any good at all, it starts to climb under its own momentum. Although it is a relatively expensive process to manipulate the British charts, the influence of the chart in the rest of the world is highly significant (especially in the giant American market) and, when placed alongside the potential earnings from overseas markets, the investment in target marketing to these 650 shops is very low indeed.

The concept of dealer bribery is neat and it is undetectable in the chart figures because its influence is indirect. Just giving records and merchandizing material away to dealers won't get a record in the charts, of course; there are many strings attached to such a deal. Many dealers are not corrupt, but the concept of what is and what is not dishonest, is always moulded by the accepted practices of the society in which an individual lives. For dealers who do take favours from distributors there are always commitments which have to be met in return. The major contribution they have to make is in-store promotion; the dealer who plays along with manipulation is usually committed to a major window display plus other items such as posters, dump bins, mobiles, merchandizing, etc.

On their own, such displays up and down the country wouldn't achieve very much. But when they are carefully timed to coincide with widescale airplay (much of it bought with cocaine), massive advertising and editorial coverage in the music press and other below-the-line marketing activities such as national fly posting, then the in-store availability and the shop displays have a definite and direct effect on which records are bought.

It is now impossible to walk into an ordinary record shop and expect to find average new releases available behind the counter. Record shops are told by the reps which records are 'priority' and no dealer who understands his business will waste time stocking any of the other 'also ran' releases.

The question then arises as to why do record companies bother releasing the also-ran records, the titles they know are *not* going to make it even before release? First, all of these losers are vital to maintain the illusion that only a small percentage of records make it, thus clearly indicating that it's not all a big fix and the public chooses what it likes and what it doesn't. Secondly, some releases are training for producers, artists, managers, and other personnel against the moment when they are ready to become 'priority'; thirdly, others are for political reasons — perhaps to please an influential manager. There are many other reasons, including the occasional genuine feeling for a record. Now and again one of the 'losers' breaks through. The Flying Pickets achieved it at the end of 1983 with a cover of the fine Yazoo song, *Only You*. The record wasn't scheduled to be 'priority', only a small number of singles were pressed in the beginning and everyone reckoned without the groundswell support that the Pickets had developed during years of constant touring. They made it the old-fashioned way and proved it could still be done, but their record was an exception and the surprise in the business was widespread.

It costs record companies about 50p to produce an album and the most expensive element — once the recording cost has been amortized — is the cardboard sleeve and printing. Giving away products worth 50p each is an expensive business when conducted on a national scale, but this is precisely what occurs every week as new 'priority' records are released. In March 1984 EMI records were fined £10,000 by the British Phonographic Institute for breaching the code laid down for the marketing of records. The company's reps had been offering dealers boxes of albums by major star names (rumoured to include Queen) and the number of free copies given depended on the chart position achieved by the singles currently being promoted.

EMI paid their fine without quibble, offered a couple of flimsy excuses and hoped that the business would quickly forget. It did. A month later another major investigation was underway as yet another round of 'freebie hype' was uncovered. The practice is endemic.

In September 1984 a distributor was fined £12,500 by the BPI after a representative had been caught personally entering false figures into one of the Dataport terminals in a chart shop. This is an extremely crude and dangerous method of chart rigging as direct phoney returns can be spotted on the computer analysis conducted by Gallup. Nevertheless such activities continue and only serve to indicate how much of the iceberg remains invisible.

Direct chart-fixing still takes place, but it is much harder to achieve these days. The Gallup charts – 7-inch singles, 12-inch singles, LPs and cassettes – are compiled weekly from 255 shops scattered around Great Britain. Three types of shop are included in the survey and these are: specialist chain stores (HMV, Our Price, Virgin, etc), multiple chain stores (Woolworth, W.H. Smith, Boots, etc) and independent shops.

When Gallup took over the compilation of the charts in January 1983 they installed special 'Dataport Retailer' terminals in every shop used in the chart survey. These intelligent terminals sit beside the tills in the chosen outlets and are connected to the shop's telephone line (incidentally providing a firm visual clue as to which shops supply chart statistics and which don't!). Every single record or tape sale made in the shop is entered by catalogue number onto the terminal where it is stored in memory.

At night, between the hours of midnight and 8am, Gallup's central computer rings round the terminals and down-loads information about the previous day's trading. The shop terminals include a clock and the computer can check on the pattern of sales entries to ensure that it fits the usual profile. Thus a dealer who decided to add an extra ten copies of a Spandau Ballet record (for instance) on a Friday afternoon, would, if he had been careless in the way he entered the bogus sales, find the unusual sales pattern showing up in the computer records. Gallup have the right to disregard any information it considers 'ambiguous' and to investigate if it thinks there has been any serious abuse of the system.

On the face of it, this seems like a pretty good system, especially when it is considered that Gallup use a 'back-up' panel of a further 400 dealers who submit postal returns, which are used to verify the swings in sales which show up in the main poll. In addition Gallup has a small team of under-cover investigators touring shops on the look-out for any breaches of the chart code.

But even though the Gallup operation has made chart fixing more difficult, it still occurs on a national scale. The Gallup computer program which collates all of the sales returns is sophisticated enough to spot unusual sales patterns emerging and can alert the chart compilation team to an attempted 'buy-in'. If, after investigation and a check with the back-up panel of shops, Gallup feel that a record is registering suspect sales, it is arbitrarily removed from the chart.

This technique makes it difficult for the old-fashioned buy-in hype to work. Some chart shops even report 'suspicious' customers to Gallup and this combination of chart analysis and dealer watchfulness serves to indicate that the industry is working hard to be pure. The fact is that the new techniques have merely made it impossible for the cowboys who operate on the fringes of the business to secure hit placings and have handed more control to the eight principal distributors who, by the combination of marketing methods described earlier, can decide which records will become hits.

Even in 1984, however, there were still a couple of 'buy in' teams operating in Britain. These groups are prepared to travel the country buying selected records on behalf of management companies who have to part with £1,500 or so a week. Usually these 'amateur' attempts at chart rigging fail and the manager (usually fairly amateur himself) is left with a disqualified record and a much depleted bank balance.

The chart itself used to be compiled from release sheets maintained by dealers and, in years gone by, I've accompanied a record company rep when he's leaned over the counter and nudged the dealer: 'Go on, give us a few more ticks then.' Those false ticks were often entered merely for friendship, not because the rep was buying them. Today the business has hardened and Gallup's tighter regulations are actually making the fixes more sophisticated and, in some instances, more profound and far reaching.

The proof that fixing occurs is provided by the fact that Gallup regularly remove Dataports from dealers and have to strike them off the chart panel. Two dealers were struck off in July 1984 for making false entries but this only reflects those who botch the fixing. The majority of false returns are extremely sohisticated and extremely difficult to spot. The major distributors are as familiar with the sales pattern of a breaking record as Gallup are and can create their own computer programs which tell them how many records should be selling in which geographic areas in order for a break to appear natural.

Getting caught is always regarded as the worst offence in the music business — far worse than carrying out a little chart tickle.

In September 1984 a sales rep working for IDS — probably the biggest independent record distributor in the country — was actually caught on the wrong side of a record shop counter keying false sales figures into Gallup's Dataport.

The BPI levied a 'fine' of £12,500 on IDS, the industry made dismayed noises about 'not tolerating interference' and both the BPI and IDS declared themselves jolly pleased that the offender had been caught and punishment meted out!

At the bottom of the Top 100, a new entry record only sells one or two a week in each shop (against 100 or so a week, on average, for a Top Ten single) and those who are good at manipulating the charts are careful not to overdo their controlling hand. With concentration on air-play and music paper promotion a record will often arrive at the lower end of the charts without any 'dishonest' fixing and then the distributor's reps can wade in with the merchandizing material and 'special' records to increase the momentum.

Records are not the only incentives offered to dealers to stock and promote records. T-shirts and similar items are now fair game and if, as happened with Frankie Goes to Hollywood, the spin-off items themselves gain a currency value then the power of the distributor over the dealer is so much greater, even though the Gallup code forbids the 'free' trade in such items.

THE VIDEO

Apart from the 'street-level' manipulation of the charts public taste is mostly bent by the relatively new marketing vehicle, the video. The video first appeared in the mid-1970s, when Queen were the first group really to exploit the commercial possibilities of making a video to promote record sales for the single *Bohemian Rhapsody*.

The idea of using film clips to promote record sales dates back to the 1930s; American juke boxes of the 1950s frequently used short films to illustrate the music. By the early 1970s Britain's main national TV outlet for rock music, Top of the Pops, was featuring films quite regularly, but the concept of using videos didn't break until 1975. Now, it is the video which is the main vehicle for the message.

The advantage for the record companies and pluggers is that a video screening presents precisely the type of image required for an act. There is no risk of having the act exposed as being anything less than hugely talented. Up until the acceptance of the video by British and American TV channels, lower-end chart success had to be followed by live, or semi-live appearances on TV by the artist. This meant that artists had to perform their numbers again in a TV studio — an environment far more hostile than the recording studio — and the visual presentation of the act was left to a TV director who an hour before may well have been directing a regional news programme. He wouldn't worry about using a poor angle on the lead singer and such details as lighting were left to chance.

Sometimes TV appearances even demanded that a band had to play live in the studio! Years of negotiations with the Musicians' Union have produced conflicting rules over live appearances: at certain periods bands had to play live (either on air or for the master taping) if they were to appear. At other times they were allowed to pre-record the backing track (but only in the TV studio — they couldn't bring along their own backing tapes) but they had to sing live vocals over them. On other occasions full miming was allowed but, usually, only to tracks recorded in the TV studio, not to the actual record itself.

TV sound is notoriously poor. Despite the fact that TV studios are blessed with high-quality sound equipment, everyone in TV is obsessed with visuals, and if you want to find out just how bad TV sound is, turn your set away from you during a live music show and listen to the sound quality. It's a wonder we've stood for it for so long.

Under this sort of onslaught, the market manipulators have now found a way to present their act in precisely the way they choose. Videos are made like small-scale feature films with budgets anywhere between £25,000 and 1,000,000. This sort of carefully controlled promotion avoids the dangers of new stars being revealed as instrumental incompetents and manages to avoid showing any less than flattering physical characteristics. If you think back over the charts of the past few years, you will be able to spot those acts which have been primarily promoted via video and which have had little or no live exposure. The video allows poor acts to be sustained in the business whereas, previously, lack of talent would fairly quickly expose poor-quality, over-hyped acts for what they were.

The advent of the video has had another dramatic effect on the international pop business. When the medium first began to be explored, it was British bands and British video directors who led the way. Readers who have spent any time in the USA will know how bad American television and TV advertising is. Despite having the world's finest film industry, the country has the worst creative advertising in the world. I consider British videos — many of them directed by award-winning directors from the world of advertising — far superior to their American counterparts. Moreover, I think the medium gave outstanding British commercial directors a chance to do something different — and the result was stunning.

The explosion of the British video as an art form coincided with the arrival of MTV, the American cable-TV channel which pumps out music 24 hours a day. This station started in 1980 and since then, the majority of its output has been British videos. The American material offered to the station just didn't compare with the excitement, the creativity and the glamour contained in the British product and, as a result, British artists took the American charts by storm. This trend has continued and it has led to an American renaissance for British talent which has surpassed even the giant British invasion of the American industry which followed the Beatles in 1964.

MTV and the British video took the American record business by surprise and it took several years for the companies to find the directing talent required to respond with sufficient power to make an impact. The 1984 video of *Thriller*, made to promote the Michael Jackson single and album, took a million dollars to make, a lot of money to spend on winning back some of the ground that British groups had won with productions made in three-day shoots in London's Limehouse and which typically only cost £25,000.

Billions of dollars flowed into the British recording industry as a result of this phenomenon and British acts now account for around a quarter of all chart singles sold in the USA. It is for this reason that the British music business is now so tightly controlled. The stakes have become tremendous.

The message is clear; no new recording artist who aims to make a hit should consider any deal which doesn't guarantee video promotion once a record starts to move.

THE CLOSED MARKET

The British pop music market can now be regarded as 'closed'. The attempts by such bodies as the BBC and Gallup to create a fairer and more representative chart have backfired and produced a situation in which target marketing and promotion have produced a chart which is less accessible to new talent than ever before — unless that new talent has the backing of one of the few giant distributors. The cost of 'hyping' a record into the charts has trebled in the last three years, and on the whole only the record companies can afford to do it.

Instead of creating an atmosphere of artistic freedom in which merit is allowed to surface, the British pop music establishment has developed a system which can be closely controlled by a few immensely rich record companies. It is to no one's advantage — least of all the long-term advantage of the record companies — that new talent is so stifled; it is to be hoped that the communications revolution of the late eighties — such as Cable TV, satellite TV broadcasts, etc — break this current, unacceptable monopoly of musical expression.

2

FORMING THE RIGHT SORT OF ACT

Now that you know that little happens by accident in the pop music business, you can begin to plan precisely how you can make a record which doesn't just get released, but which becomes a HIT!

The all-powerful vehicle of the video demands that the first element you should consider is your image. In the old days, 'image' used to be a joke word: if a band like the Honeycombs had a girl drummer, that was an 'image'. Sandie Shaw's image, or gimmick to use a better word, was to perform barefoot. Gilbert O'Sullivan dressed up as a schoolboy to promote his first three singles. The business thrives on such nonsense. But in the past the image, or gimmick, was quickly dropped after it had served its purpose of grabbing attention. Today image is a much more serious affair.

Image is now perpetuated to an almost alarming extent. Perhaps the best examples of modern image building have been Boy George and Culture Club, and Frankie Goes to Hollywood. Boy George's absurd male/female hybrid image fitted its time precisely: sexual demarcation is under constant attack, not only in the world of the young, but in the far more serious real world of the genetic laboratory. Boy George, for all that he was flippant and commercially promoted, was saying something about our times.

Frankie Goes To Hollywood was treated to a far more subtle marketing campaign. The image that what 'Frankie Says' matters was developed partly by luck and partly by manipulation. 'Arm The Unemployed' was the sort of anarchist statement which appealed to those who only had to support the concept at T-shirt level and the phenomenon of the Frankie re-mix singles and T-shirt in the summer of 1984 was certainly one of the most cynical pieces of marketing the British pop music business has yet seen. Fans were persuaded to buy several records of the same song — each with a slightly different sound mix – and a brief fashion developed for wearing T-shirts which quoted the 'wisdom' of Frankie on a wide variety of topics.

CHOOSING THE IMAGE

Image is all: whatever you decide to become, if you are lucky and determined, will be developed and magnified a thousandfold by the powerful medium of television and video. You will need to stand out, to be different, no matter how great your musical talent. Once you have decided on your style, the most important lesson of all is to learn *to live it with your whole heart.*

Even the Beatles had gimmicks: the mop-top hair cuts and the suits without collars were as outrageous in their day as Boy George's transvestism. But being outrageous isn't necessarily the key to developing a successful image. There are several heavy metal bands who go in for stunts such as biting heads off chickens and other unsavoury on-stage antics, but none of that is going to make them anything but distasteful paragraph news for the cheaper tabloid newspapers. Every newspaper demands an 'angle' for every story, something that turns it into 'news'. The fact that you've released your first single after four years of trying may be the biggest news in your life but it won't make a Fleet Street features editor sit up and shout for joy: in fact, you wouldn't even get a mention.

With artists such as Boy George and Marilyn adopting such extreme styles it is hard to imagine what can come next, but someone will always go one better: perhaps by rejecting an extreme and going for something more subtle but perhaps equally powerful.

FOLLOWING A FASHION

One of the main complaints of producers and talent scouts is that all of the new bands and singers seem to style themselves on those artists who are already successful. 'Oh, he's just another Howard Jones, or Thomas Dolby'. The moment someone makes such a comment about you, you've had it. No matter how well you sing, play or write songs, your act is debased as far as that producer or manager is concerned. You mustn't be a look-alike or sound-alike.

We are all fans and we are all influenced by those singers, songwriters and musicians we particularly like. The danger is that it is all too easy to become clones. Being 'influenced' by a particular artist or group is a long and worthy tradition in music, but the problem is working out where 'influence' stops and becoming 'derivative' begins.

Some copy-cats have been wildly successful. Cliff Richard copied Elvis Presley unashamedly in the late 1950s and has since built quite a reasonable career for himself (after evolving his own image). Donovan became Britain's 'answer' (the euphemism the business uses for copies) to Bob Dylan in the 1960s and his career was OK for a while. Others have copied since and some will go on doing so successfully, but it is far safer to develop your own particular image.

The question about following a fashion or not is a difficult one: sometimes a fashion, a 'mood', can last several years and during that period dozens of artists within that genre can make it. The problem is that the fashion cycle in the music business is speeding up. The evidence of the first half of the 1980s is that a current fashion has a maximum life of about two years.

If you arrive early in a new musical or cultural movement it is possible to follow others into the charts with the same fashion underlying your image. If the fashion is nearing the end of its run (a very difficult thing to decide) it is dangerous, if not suicidal to form a band which plays the same sort of music and looks similar to those who are currently dominating the charts.

Perhaps the best guideline is to ask yourself whether or not you were playing that type of music and dressing or performing that type of way before it became fashionable. If you were, you are probably in the vanguard of the movement and you should stick with it. If you see the new style and hear the new sounds for the first time on

'The Tube' or on 'Top of the Pops' you should forget about it. Rehearsing copy-cat material which you've already seen exploited on video and TV is asking to die artistically. Yet so many do it!

DECIDING WHAT YOU DO BEST

The very best images are developments of your own personality. Your face might be your greatest asset. By that I don't mean that you have to be stunningly good-looking (although that can be an advantage). I mean that if your face is unusual, out of the ordinary, it can be very useful as something on which to capitalize. Unusual and interesting faces can be every bit as eye-catching as startling good looks.

Outstanding good looks can actually be a problem. Young men, in particular, can suffer in the music business by being 'too pretty'. Michael Jackson seems to contradict these statements by his Peter Pan image, but the number of times I have heard managers and record companies worrying over a boy singer who is 'too pretty' has convinced me that it can be a definite curse as well as a blessing.

There are fashions in what is considered good looking. In the late fifties the sultry looks of Presley were deemed the ultimate. In the mid-1960s the sort of openness suggested by Paul McCartney's and Peter Frampton's faces were the rage, whereas in the early 1970s the vulnerable, elfin look of David Essex and Marc Bolan reflected public taste. Just after the punk revolution of 1976 'street' faces were in: these *couldn't* be good looking: if they were they were suspect.

Today we have a broad canvas of acceptable looks and those who are traditionally good looking are acceptable again. But prettiness can be a problem, and if you or one of your band has a face that is 'saccharin sweet' you should do your best to develop an image and clothes style which hardens rather than softens it. Personal objectivity is desperately hard, of course, but as you are planning to place yourself in front of millions on a regular basis, it is better for you to try and appraise precisely who and what you are before your audiences do it for you — possibly supplying the wrong answer!

Other than plastic surgery, the use of which is not unknown by some stars, there's nothing any of us can do about our face.

Be careful when deciding how far to push your fashion image. There have been several semi-successful bands who have made it while sporting really outrageous styles such as shaved heads, but there is a limit to the psychological acceptability which finally governs their mass appeal.

It would be hard to think of anything seemingly more outrageous than Boy George, but once you look further into his early image you will realize that it proved pleasing and easy on the eye. The ugly just will not work on the mass of record buyers.

Try and pick a look with appeal. Avoid overt sexuality if you are female or if there's a girl in your band: with the exception of Tina Turner, Janis Joplin, The Pointer Sisters, Donna Summer and a few others, most female pop performers have failed to sell sex and maintain musical integrity. There's a definite conflict and any sexual style should come out of the natural exhibitionism of the performer rather than a manager's (or fellow musician's) idea of what is required. It's an area best avoided if you're at all unsure.

If you are serious about making it in the pop business (and you're not as broke as most hopefuls) don't dismiss the idea of cosmetic surgery to correct a flaw or to improve a particular feature. Be cautious in this area, however. Most hopeful pop artists and young people lack one important quality: perspective. What might seem a right move to fit in with the mood of the times may well prove disastrous in ten years time. Ask those with forehead tatoos, nose rings or pierced nipples: fun in King's Road 1978, appalling in Gateshead in the middle eighties.

The biggest problem in embarking on cosmetic surgery is finding someone you can trust. A family who cares about you is a good source of information, but if there's a massive generation gap you may not get objective opinions from worried fathers or mothers.

Good cosmetic surgeons are hard to find, principally because they have to be designers as well. It is not good enough to be skilful with the scalpel; the cosmetic surgeon has got to have an instinctive 'eye' for what will look right. If he or she is unable to imagine how you'll look after your cheekbones are sharpened, then they won't be able to design you a very nice face.

HIT TIP

WARNING: Don't embark on anything as drastic as cosmetic surgery unless you are absolutely certain it will make all the difference to your career. If you've got an awful nose which you think wrecks an otherwise lovely face, you may be destroying a wonderful asset if you have it re-shaped. That nose might be the identifier which marks you out from all the other 'pretties'.

In your face, your body, your personality, your clothes and your music, try to find elements that are quintessentially YOU. If you have humour, exploit it, don't hide it just because it's currently fashionable to be dead serious. If you're very serious about your musicality, make that a major feature of the act, of your own personality. Don't be persuaded that it is less important than a hair style. If your fashion sense is your greatest asset follow your own instincts about dress and don't let managers or anybody else persuade you to wear something that you know is wrong. In all, be yourself, but remember that the pop music business demands that once you have found out what you are you have to magnify it many times over.

FINDING OTHERS TO WORK WITH

Singers who wish to work alone can ignore this section. Most singers and musicians want to work with others and finding the right people to work with can be very, very hard.

Make sure that you've worked out who you are before you start playing regularly with another group of hopefuls. You might easily get sucked into someone else's ideas if you're not certain what yours are. On occasions this can work, of course: if you have no clear idea about yourself and have been unable to develop an objective view, then there's no harm in blending into and adding to the persona that has been developed within an existing group. Many successful musicians have done just that: Helen Terry, Alison Moyet, George Harrison, Bill Wyman, Jimmy Page, Ian Warr, Martin Barre have all proved they can emerge from the shadow of a larger image and develop their own separate identities. If you're not ready to put your stamp on others, don't feel ashamed to hitch your wagon onto a good tow.

One important lesson must be learned when you are finding others to play with: don't expect to find them living in the same street as you. It is natural for you to want to play with friends. If you're a drummer and your best friend plays a synthesizer, it's understandable that you will want to play together. There's nothing wrong with that, so long as you realize that giant talents aren't to be found on every street. Most 'local' groups have one, or at the most, two, good members and the rest are the 'also rans' who happened to be friends of the prime movers. This type of structure is fine for a 'fun' band, a group just out to have a few laughs, but if you want to make hit records, you're going to have to get a bit tougher in your attitudes and start casting around for real talent to play with.

ADVERTISING

Don't be afraid to advertise. Most young people are nervous of using advertisements to find other musicians to work with, in case they won't be good enough to play with the people who respond, or they won't be liked. But actually they are just apprehensive about putting themselves on the line.

This is where you have to make your first decision on the hard road which will take you to the charts. Are you ruthless enough to fire a member of your band who is clearly holding you back? The Beatles fired Pcte Best when George Martin felt he wasn't good enough. Pete had been with the group two years, through all their Hamburg days. It has now been revealed that the Beatles had already started to have their own misgivings about him, but could you do that?

There's nothing nice or good about being ruthless, but you'll have to steel yourself to do unpleasant things if you *really* want to make it. The road from obscurity to stardom is strewn with obstacles: each one will demand that you compromise a little of your integrity. As a well known keyboard player once put it: 'My integrity is being held by my bank manager as collateral'. If you can't take the hard decisions, you won't make it.

It is unreasonable to expect to find the country's best musicians living in your home town – unless that happens to be London or Glasgow or one of our other major cities. If you live in a small town, you must expect to look further afield to find people who are compatible with you musically and who you enjoy playing with.

Be careful that you don't opt for the comfort of just playing with 'mates': if you're serious about creating a successful band, you'll have to be a little bit ruthless in chasing quality. Many 'local' bands fail simply because they are too nice to each other. There's often a passenger: a singer who can't really sing, a guitarist who's just there because he has a van, or a drummer who 'started' the group.

If you're really serious about building an act that will make a hit your aims can be broken down into phases. These are:

1 Create an act that is different *and* good.
2 Hone it in front of audiences (if your's is to be a performing band).
3 Find a *good*, successful manager (optional — see chapter on management).
4 Secure a *good* record deal.
5 Capture your style on record.
6 Promote the record as hard as you can.
7 Make a good video.
8 Enter the charts.

Setting the aims out on paper makes them seem ridiculously easy: to a young synthesizer player desperately trying to interface a BBC micro with a Roland synth, it might seem just fatuous. But this is precisely how a major record company views the process of breaking new acts and they set about achieving Phases 5 to 8 in a very calculated way.

No matter where you are in the business, you should consider holding auditions to find other musicians you wish to play with. If you do have one other person in whom you're confident that is a major step forward, but never be frightened about the idea of playing with people who are better than you musically. Your concept of what you're doing, your business ability (if you have any) and your determination to succeed can make up for the fact that a musician you audition may be more accomplished than you are. All successful bands are an amalgam of talent, style, determination, shrewdness and, of course, luck.

You may be lucky and find a strong nucleus for your band fairly easily. You will certainly need at least two, and possibly three people, who share similar musical tastes, who play well together and have common aims. Outside that 'inner circle' it is possible to have others who are simply band members; here there is an important first principal to be established.

It is impossible to teach experience; that is why vulnerable, hopeful kids will always fall prey to the experienced, persuasive sharks of the music business. One thing you can try to imagine, however, is how the established music business moguls judge talent.

If your musical experience is limited to school, college and playing with mates on the local circuit, you're likely to have a very one-dimensional view of what is good and what is bad. Quite simply, you won't have heard enough live music to have any objectivity about yourself.

The best way to overcome this is to listen to as many records as possible in an analytical way, rather than just for enjoyment. Equally important is getting out to see other bands perform: this can be the greatest education of all. Even if you don't like a particular act, watching their show with a professional eye can earn you many tips and hints which you can adapt and translate to your own needs.

The record company talent scout who will eventually listen to your demo or visit a club to see you will have been hearing bands and singers for years. Most likely, he started out like you, in a band, as a hopeful and since those early days he'll have listened to thousands of young bands all over Britain, America and Europe. He has the experience to compare what you are doing to thousands of others stored in his memory. You might be good at what you do, but he may have heard bands do it better in Berlin, Washington or Glasgow.

It is impossible to provide you with a twenty year overview of the business in a few paragraphs, but it will definitely be helpful if you recognize the yawning gap that will exist between you and him. He won't look much older than you when he comes backstage or when you meet him across a desk, but you should be aware that musically he's from another planet. Bear this in mind when you are creating your act: any hint of copying, of derivative behaviour, in music or stage act, will earn you rejection. His standards are much, much higher than yours.

All young people are by nature democratic. The young like fair play more than any other group in society. As a result the natural arrangement for young bands is to agree to do everything unanimously. The result is chaos.

It's quite an old fashioned idea to have a 'leader' of a group, but although that term is no longer used, the concept has come back into fashion very strongly in the 1980s.

One or two people in the band must make the majority of the day-to-day decisions. In the early flush of excitement in finding a combination of musicians which works, it is easy to believe in the Utopian ideal of a fully democratic band structure: to an extent the musicians see themselves as united against all enemies, usually the managers, agents, producers, promoters and all others ready to rip them off. In practice this is rarely a successful form of organization.

You will have to decide whether you are a leader or a follower by nature: not an easy decision. Regrettably the world is divided into these two categories, with a sizeable minority which hovers in between, but in the very close and intimate family of a band, the pecking order has to be established very quickly if the band is to survive their first bout of real pressure.

Playing a few local gigs won't impose any more strain than the typical complaints that the bass player hasn't paid his share of the petrol money or that the drummer was late. This is normal and can safely be ignored. If you are serious about making hit records you've got to look beyond this.

The pressures on even a semi-successful band are frightening. When you visit Manchester it is likely that both Granada TV and the *Manchester Evening News* will want an interview. The democrats share this out, allowing two members to get the more glamorous TV interview in one town, and trading it with the others in another. This is likely to be to the detriment of the band's career. As mentioned earlier, most bands have a nucleus, a couple of main movers, often the front men or women on stage. These are the characters with whom the public identify most and although it may bruise the ego of the drummer and other back-line players, it would be harmful if these important faces stepped out of the important Granada TV slot (usual evening viewing two million) just because it wasn't their turn.

Many egos get bruised on the way to international success and heavy money and if you're a back-line member, always remember that is your role: trying to move forward into the limelight too early will wreck everybody's chance. Equally, if you are a front man, insist on being so. This is just one more of those 'hard' decisions that have to be made and stuck to on the road to success.

WHOSE BAND IS IT?

This question has to be worked out from Day One. If you don't, if you play it nice, you'll get caught out. If you write the songs, if you're the lead singer, if the band is your concept, then you have a claim that the band belongs to you — perhaps in partnership with one or two others. If you've joined someone else's concept, remember it was theirs and no matter how great your contribution, save any move towards a greater share in the glory (or the money — see below) until the band is established.

It is a good idea to register the ownership of a band's name. In the old days all you had to do was register it as a business name — it cost £1. Today it is more difficult to place ownership on a name. You actually need to develop a 'logo', a special print style of name which can become a registered trademark, and it might be a good idea to form a limited company with the same name; you will certainly need legal advice on this point.

HOW TO SPLIT THE MONEY

Most successful groups which split up do so over money. The reasons given in the press are usually rubbish: 'We wanted to develop in different directions', 'I wanted to concentrate on my solo career'. You can interpret most of these fatuous statements as meaning 'I was getting screwed'.

There are, of course, occasions when bands do break up for artistic or practical reasons, but most of the time it comes down to money and it usually occurs because the financial situation wasn't made clear *before* the band started to make money.

The usual pattern of events is that a band gets together with only the vaguest idea about financial structure. Because there is absolutely no money available within an unsuccessful band it seems totally pointless to develop contracts which define the split between the members. When the band does get a hit it seems as though the world explodes: from having no money, the stuff is everywhere. Chauffeur-driven limos purr at the kerbside day and night; champagne and coke are always on the dressing table; any instrument, any car, any trip: all is possible. In the white heat of success, very often the first time the young members of a band have had any taste of real money, it is not surprising that 'who gets what' is forgotten in the euphoria of having made it. During this period the entire band will, quite likely, get ripped off: by managers, agents, producers and even record companies. That's the nature of the game. It is reasonable to assume that any bunch of poor young people faced with adulation and piles of money will be completely unable to control the situation and will willingly hand over all responsibility for the 'boring' figurework to those with the experience, while the kids get on with having the 'good time' so long denied to them because of their class and lack of money. In the first two years much of what they earn may well be stolen from them.

The subject of the management rip-off is covered in much more detail later in the book, but it is after this initial buzz has worn off and the band members get down to counting what is left that real bitterness can set in and cause rows over money.

It is impossible to turn an eighteen-year-old keyboard player into an international accountant, but more and more young musicians are now realizing the importance of structuring their careers carefully right from the start and are employing their own accountants and lawyers on a retainer basis from the moment they are offered their first record deal.

Although it is hard to expect a young musician to be capable of financial prudence, it may be possible to persuade him to strike a deal with the other members of the band so that they all know what cut they will be getting. Imagine a new five piece band getting together in Newcastle. The front men are two singers and song-writers who have been together for two years. Now the time has come to build a group as a vehicle for the songs and image they have developed. How should the earnings from the band be split?

It is true that if the front men write all the songs, the income they will get from a hit success will be much more than the other non-songwriting members of the band: but does this make it equitable for all other income to be split equally five ways? The sensible musicians think this one out before the first demo is ever laid down.

A successful band earns a fortune. A band with three number one singles both sides of the Atlantic (and spin-off successes in other world territories) and with two international Top Ten albums, can earn several hundred million dollars gross inside three years. The money comes from recording and songwriting royalties, tour earn-ings, video sales, merchandizing and associated exploitations. The important difference is the meaning between the words *gross* and *net*. How much the net figure is — the important one for the artist — entirely depends on the management and/or record deal (dis-cussed later).

As already mentioned, much of this money is likely to be ripped off, or at least lost to the band. You may be able to avoid this if you are careful, but it is an endemic evil of the music business and only if you are very smart indeed will you be able to avoid the worst excesses of the financial vultures who gather around new stars.

The smart move is to spot when you may be ripped off, control the extent of this thievery, plan for the 'discovery' when the band finds itself world-famous but underpaid and then use the fame that no one can take from you to build a career for life.

It was relatively easy to write that last paragraph: achieving its aims is phenomenally difficult and only a few, very bright performers have succeeded. But you can minimize the havoc of big money arriving fast. The first rule is to sort out the split within the band *before* you get a chance to make it.

When there's no money about it is easy to agree to split everything equally, In the five-piece band mentioned above, it would be tempting and easy to agree to share all costs and earnings equally: indeed, in the early stages of a band's life it is the only way it could work. But if you are one of the two front men, you should consider getting a partnership or limited company agreement drawn up which spells out what will happen after you start earning certain sums of money. Doing this will reveal you as a calculating, money-grabbing business person. Not doing it could smash up the act into which you are putting your life and soul. The answer is to do it, but to try to do it softly and gently so no one takes fright.

One suggestion is to agree to share all costs and all earnings equally up until the point where all band members are earning at least £500 per week. To musicians used to £34 a week dole money such a suggestion will seem ridiculous: to musicians who are seriously planning to make hit records, the dole is only a stepping stone. The big time has to be planned for if it is to be enjoyed.

Agreeing a sliding scale of percentage take often works in a band of the sort described above. The back-line members know that whatever happens they'll do OK and the agreement you write should ensure that even when the act is world class, they will still be earning far more than they could by hawking the name they have achieved elsewhere. Thus the top scale (the Number One hit level) might consist of a deal which gives the two front men an equal share of 65 per cent of earnings and the rest of the band an equal share of the remaining 35 per cent — all on top of the agreed initial £500 per week. This type of deal can work very well and can survive all sorts of international money difficulties. If you do feel totally egalitarian and wish to share everything equally, you should be aware that only the rarest type of human being is generous enough to watch huge sums of money being passed to others in seemingly unfair divisions over a long period of time.

Those who receive large amounts of money to which they do not feel truly entitled also feel bad. Eventually, they will begin to imagine slights where there are none in order to off-set their guilt at ripping you off. If you're a strong enough person to get the right deal hammered out in the early days you'll never regret it.

Be very careful which lawyer you go to. Visiting the local high-street lawyer is not a good idea, unless the practice has specialized in show-business clients. You must find a lawyer who has worked with music business clients before and is used to what can go wrong inside groups. That way you'll be covered. It won't be cheap getting a good partnership agreement drawn up and if you've got no money you may have to wait until you've earned your first advance to spend the £200 or so necessary to get a good agreement drawn up. If this is the case, make a point of telling the band roughly the terms you want *at the beginning* and remind them from time to time that there will be a contract to this effect drawn up in the future.

REHEARSING

You have to decide what type of band or act you want. If you're a solo singer the decision isn't so hard, but bands should think long and hard about how they are going to break into the business before setting up the act. There are two main routes:

A To form a working band, play as many gigs as possible and then arrive at a point ready to record.

B Decide from the beginning that you're going to start out as a studio band.

The last option has only recently become viable in the music business, even though studio bands have been making hits for 30 years. The reason they were previously always one-hit wonders — such as The Archies or Love Affair — is that they weren't able to exploit the only means of promotion open to them — going on the road. Now the video has provided a means of promotion just as powerful as a national tour, but which does not demand that the band is able to play together in public.

Getting a band good on stage, 'tight' as they say in the business, is so hard it is almost unbelievable. The hurdles that have to be overcome are described later in this book, but you should think very carefully before deciding whether you really want to play live.

If you opt for what seems the easy option of starting as a studio band — in the way that bands like Frankie Goes To Hollywood and Duran Duran started — you face different problems which are equally difficult to overcome. You will have to replace the touring slog with money. There will still be plenty of musical slog, but you won't have to face the awful nights loading the van at the back of Wallasey Town Hall at 2am in the driving rain. If, however, you think Wallasey, or at least touring, has its attractions, then the answer is obvious: perhaps you just want to be on stage and pull the girls — if so, enjoy yourself, but you aren't likely to have the single-minded determination necessary to ensure you start making hits.

Money is required for a studio band in order that high-standard studio production can be made and an initial video developed, sometimes before a record deal is concluded. It isn't as hard to raise money to finance pop groups today as it was in the past, since it is possible to sell shares in a band as though it were a newly-formed company, but this only applies *if* you have an experienced lawyer or manager.

DO YOU NEED A MANAGER?

Nowadays many bands never have a manager, while others have one from the outset. If you're going to form a band and start playing as many gigs as possible you don't need to think about management. What you will need is a first class hustler who can get the gigs for you. That person will probably not demean himself by calling himself an agent, but will want to be called your 'manager' and take 25 per cent of your gross earnings. If you find someone who can get gigs (which is down to nothing but persistent telephone hustling), you should treat him in the same way he will plan to treat you.

Tell him how delighted you are to have him as a manager. Don't show any dismay at the appalling, lousy contract he'll hand you — he's bound to want to tie you up for ten years without allowing you any control over your career or money. Whatever you do, *Don't sign it*, but stall as long as you can, make him prove that he's tough enough to fill your date sheet, and then play the nice/nasty act on him as he would on you if he got the chance.

Once given the contract, go and see an experienced show business lawyer and tell the lawyer bluntly that you want to *use* this manager on the way up. Tell him that you want to hide behind him as the nice innocent musician whose rotten solicitor won't let them sign the contract as it stands. You'll have to box very cleverly to hang onto your gig hustler while these difficult negotiations are going on (they should last months, by the way) but if he plays true to form he will get you even more gigs during this period to prove just how good he is.

You must not sign a long term agreement with this hustler unless he has proved he can manage hit acts: this does not mean that he managed one act which had a hit three years ago. It must mean that he has managed several acts which have had a string of Top Five hits in the last two years or, at the very minimum, one major act which has managed to sustain itself for at least three hits.

It is very unlikely that the sort of local gig hustler you're likely to come across in your early days will fall into this category. It is far more likely that he'll be a hip version of a double-glazing salesman who is either a failed musician or someone who is vicariously attracted to the so-called glamour of the music business. If he's in either of these categories, you must 'use' him without compunction, for this is precisely what he will intend to do to you. When the time comes, and you've got your experience and reputation and you attract a successful manager (or decide to handle the business yourselves), you've got to be able to politely decline his future services immediately and sign with the major management house or conclude the record deal. You may still be ripped off by your new manager, of course, (more of that later), but you'll be ripped off with your career well handled instead of failing to make it altogether.

If you do, by chance, come across a good local manager who is genuinely caring, a nice guy and someone you can trust, *give him the boot now!* You'll do him no favours by working with him and he won't be in a position to do you any. Remember, it's now been revealed that even 'nice' Brian Epstein was just trying to get into John Lennon's pants and his motivation in getting the Beatles the break was not at all altruistic.

The nice guy without the experience *cannot* get you the break. The little shit who hustles clubs up and down the country can; use him. If it's getting to the point where you'll either have to sign something or break off with your gig supplier (and there's no major deal in sight) get your lawyer to put in all sorts of break clauses in the contract which will limit your ties to a year. This means that when the offer comes, the new manager or record label will be able to buy you out of your contract quite cheaply.

The sort of break clauses which are effective include: 'if at the end of the first twelve months the artist has not earned a minimum of £10,000 *net*, the contract shall be considered void . . . .', or 'if at the end of twelve months the artist shall not have released a record which has entered the BBC/Gallup charts at a position higher than twenty . . . ' etc, etc. An experienced music business lawyer will be able to come up with all sorts of lovely suggestions. You may lose your lovely gig-hustler, but it's better than handing him five years of your career and giving away your chance of success.

Going on the road demands all sorts of money: doing it at a strictly small club level now demands about £7,500 excluding transport, and this really is doing it on the cheap. Most band members are likely to bring about £1,000 worth of gear with them (averaged out), but it's the cost of the front-line PA and mixer which is likely to prove prohibitive. The answer is to hire, just as you would transport. Don't consider sinking £3,000 into a PA unless you're grossing at least £800 a week; even then, you'd be better off renting in many instances. Finding the money to fund a band is discussed later, but the last point about the junior hustler/manager is that if he's got money there may be some reason to grant slightly longer contracts. Always argue far more about the duration of the contract than the percentage points. If he's ripping you off when you're unsuccessful he's ripping you off for pennies and, although it won't seem like it to you, paying 40 per cent of next to nothing is a lot easier than paying 40 per cent of a lot. People who haven't earned much money in their lives always think about it the other way round, but it is very hard to give away 40 per cent when it represents hundreds of thousands of pounds.

Never sign an unbreakable contract of more than two years' duration with any manager who does not have the right sort of track record. If you do, you can be almost certain that you'll have to wait the length of that contract and then another couple of years before you get the chance to make a hit. Hits are artificially created, remember, and if a manager is involved he is the central pivot on which the manufacturing process lies. Don't make a wrong decision about management at an early stage of your career.

3

MAKING THE DEMO

Demonstrating how your band sounds on a demonstration recording has been a useful practice since the early days of rock 'n' roll. If Elvis hadn't made a demo for his Mom, Sam Phillips and (as a result) the world, would never have heard him.

Most record company executives, managers and producers choose to sift through would-be talent by the simple expedient of listening to demo tapes (and still, occasionally, records). It is much easier than travelling the country to listen to performing acts of whom they know nothing.

You will have to be prepared to pay hundreds and possibly thousands of pounds to fund your own demos or buy your own recording equipment before you can interest any one of these people. A demonstration recording must be just that: a clear demonstration of your talent and, in particular, of your *uniqueness*. If that doesn't come over in a demo, you need not bother spending the money on postage to send it out.

YOU WILL BE HEARD

All demos are listened to. Lots of hopeful bands put demo tapes in the post half thinking that they probably won't even get a hearing. *Every* tape does, however, as this is the only chance most producers and managers have of hearing something new or fresh. But you have to be aware of one important fact: *only the first 30 seconds of your demo will count.*

Trevor Horn, one of Britain's top producers reckons he gets 50 tapes a week to listen to. He hears them all, but if he's not hooked within half a minute, the tape is off the machine and the next one is on. This is especially true if, in that 30 seconds, he hears something that gives the band away as being hopeless, amateurish, incompetent or simply boring.

HIT TIP

Do not think about making a demo in the same way that you would think about making a master single. Making a demo demands completely different techniques to recording a track intended for air play. If your record is played on the air it will always be played in full. A demo is *never* played in full unless the first 30 seconds says something special about the band.

You must structure your recording differently for a demo from the way you would for a master. Put the 'hook' first (the hook is the chorus, for the uninitiated). If you're selling a voice or voices, get them in within ten seconds, not a moment later.

Don't have long instrumental intros. *Don't* demo a slow romantic number which takes time to build up. *Don't* allow the keyboard player to open with a long programmed sequence: give it your best shot right up front, in the reverse way to the way you would do it on stage or on a single. Then go back, do the verses and the middle eight and hit them with the hook over and over again. Relentlessly. A good demo is a parody of a proper recording: you're making a tape for a market which is totally different from the normal record buying market. Every producer and manager has heard far more music than you have and they haven't the head space for normal enjoyment. Remember most people in the music business hate most of the music they hear. If you don't impress the hell out of them the moment they start your tape, they won't run it long enough to hear the great harmonizing you may have added at the end. It's all got to be right up front.

When it comes to deciding what to record you really have no option but to record the material you write. (If you don't write any material — and why not? — see below).

The most important talent in the entire music business is the ability to write hit songs. This talent is prized above vocal and instrumental virtuosity and even above the sort of charisma shown by the greats. Those who make money and lasting success out of the business are the songwriters. Work hard to develop this side of your talent. If you are absolutely sure you can't do it, try to find someone who can and get him or her in your band *NOW*. It doesn't matter if they can't play or sing, but you need songwriting talent. Without it, you're going to have a very difficult job persuading any manager and record company to put up the £500,000 it will take to make you a hit.

The only times it is excusable not to record your own or other original material on a demonstration recording are:

1. You have a singer with a voice so outstanding that it is obviously world class (hard for you to be sure of with your limited experience).
2. Your act or visual is so outrageous that the material hardly matters (in which case you should be making a demo video and not a record — see below).
3. You have an established club reputation.
4. You have an arrangement of an old hit that is so stunning that it is likely to revive it (once again, hard for you to assess accurately with only a few years in the business).

Even if your band or track falls into one of these categories, you should still record your own material if possible. If you have recreated an old hit in a wonderful way a manager and record company are still going to ask where the follow-up hits are going to come from. Today a band without writers is like a photographer without film: pretty useless. The days of the band of travelling musicians has gone. If all you can do is play an instrument reasonably well or sing passably you're doomed to a life of endless on-the-road monotony unless you have a particularly lucky break. Whether that monotony is relatively better than the boredom of working as a clerk for the local gas board is a moot point, but in relation to the chance of becoming a star, or of making a hit, songwriting is everything.

WHAT WILL IT COST?

You can make a demo for £100 and if your song is wonderful, it might do the job. However, you should think in terms of spending at least £500 and, probably, more like £1,000 if you're going to do yourselves full justice.

To an extent cost depends on the type of band you are. If there's a large amount of pre-programming you can do, you may save a lot of studio time. If your act is largely made up of real-time instruments, you might find it takes quite a long time to get the sound you want — especially if you're not used to recording.

If you've never been into a recording studio before, the best tip is to take the songs apart before you go in to record. Rehearse them a hundred times so that you can't get them out of your mind when you're trying to sleep and then make sure every member of the band knows his or her part well enough to be able to play it entirely unaccompanied. This isn't as easy as it sounds and it is a very good test of whether you're ready to record. If you are using real-time instruments, make sure that every part is rehearsed individually as well as ensemble.

There are three types of recording studio in Britain.

1 **Bargain basement** Usually four or eight-track small format machines such as Teacs or Tascams. These studios are usually in deep financial trouble so try screwing a deal out of them rather than accepting the prices on their rate card. Many of them offer an all-day session plus master tape and two cassettes for £80 or so, but try offering them £70 and see if they'll bite. Add the fact that

you're prepared to pay up front and in cash to sweeten the deal. In some parts of the country you can do very well.

2 **Mid-range** These studios are mostly sixteen or 24-track and have serious machines such as 3Ms, Ampex or Scullys. They're likely to have some properly designed studio premises with adjustable acoustics and, perhaps, even some automated mixdown. If you haven't come across this phrase before, you should remember it. In automated mixdown, a computer is used to remember the position of the faders on each attempt at the mix. It remembers every previous move, so that as you move from Mix 1 to Mix 2 you only have to adjust those parts of the first mix you didn't like. This means that after three or four mixes you're going to be very close to having precisely the mix you want. If a studio charges an extra £5 an hour but offers automated mixdown, take it, as it will save you much more than that in mixing time.

Typical charges in mid-range studios go from £15 an hour to £30 an hour, and some offer all-day deals for bands wanting to make demos. There's less scope for doing deals in this class as the studios are usually run by more professional managers, but there's never any harm asking.

3 **The big league** If you've already got a fairy godfather or a manager you may have the financial muscle to use one of the big league studios. These charge between £60 and £100 per hour and offer almost everything.

RECORDING AT HOME

It might be worthwhile hiring an eight-track Tascam and mixing desk to record a demo in your home if you've an area suitable for acoustic treatment. The biggest problem in mobile recording is finding an area which is acoustically controllable. If you're a garage band in the literal sense, the sound inside your garage will be so awful before you adjust it that the better the recording gear you use the worse the demo will sound.

If you've got premises somewhere that you can convert — by bringing in old curtains, carpets and blankets to deaden sound reflection — careful home recording can produce a successful demo. Some hits have been made using budget multi-track tape machines, but it takes great patience and skill to keep the standard of sound quality high as the tracks are built up.

The greatest enemy of small format multi-track recording is noise: not just the noise which may occur around you while you are recording, but the noise of the tape itself. This is called background hiss and it is the sound of the tape which seems to build up every time an extra track is recorded. The best method of dealing with it is to hire a noise-reduction system, such as a Dolby or DMX, at the same time as you hire the mixer.

HIT TIP

If you've got a couple of thousand pounds in the bank, or if you can find the credit, it is a very good idea to buy an eight-track studio system as a permanent item. Secondhand Teacs and mixers can be had for this sum and the constant availability of demo-recording is very helpful for bands and songwriters.

If you buy a system you will learn how to use it over a matter of months even if you've never had any studio experience. You will need an area which you can convert and use for recording on a semi-permanent basis; this is often the biggest single problem. If such a set-up can be established, however, the cost of making demos falls dramatically and you can seriously plan to send out new demos every three months or so. Every serious songwriter should set his or her sights directly at owning a four or eight-track studio system. It is the equivalent of a word processor for a writer — invaluable.

Don't contemplate recording at home unless one of the band has had some mixing experience. Mixing takes some time to learn and judging the right relative balances of instruments and voices isn't easy. If you do have experience in mixing then an entire rig consisting of eight-track Teac, sixteen channel sound desk, noise reduction and six microphones can be hired for around £30 a day. You'll also need to hire a two-track stereo machine on which to record your final version of the mix. This will cost a further £10 to £15 a day.

FINDING THE MONEY

The big question every band faces is: is it worth going into debt? It's an impossible question to answer as a generality, but despite the understandable caution of parents, the answer, quite often, is 'yes!'

If one of your band has a day job, or has any type of securable asset you should be able to borrow the money required for a demo or a studio system from one of the High Street banks. It's easy to borrow a few thousand pounds these days and the banks are much more liberal about what they will lend money for.

There is, of course, an argument that says banks don't really want to know what it's for and by telling them a lie, you'll just be helping the person who asks the question to fill in a box on the form in a way that will satisfy his or her superiors. However, it's perfectly OK and sensible to tell them it's for buying a studio system, but accept that they might not like the idea of the loan being spent on a single recording session.

If you can't handle debt mentally, you're faced with the old-fashioned idea of saving, and as that's almost impossible for a serious band, you may need to look for a financial backer earlier than you're ready to.

The best time to seek financial input is *after* you've secured a record deal or the patronage of a successful manager (then you'll get heavy money on really good terms).

HIT TIP

If you need investment money early in your career try advertising in your local paper and in small classified boxes in such papers as the *Financial Times* and the *Investors Chronicle.* You could say something like: 'Professional recording pop group with lucrative tour opportunities, seeks investment from a financier interested in the pop music business.'

That type of advertisement will only attract inexperienced managers, but innocent investors are what you want at this stage. You're looking for the sort of investment that's offered by an over-indulgent father to his eighteen-year-old son who wants to be in a pop group. The problem with using a father's money is that you certainly can't rip him off by dumping him when the time comes (well, you could, but it would cause such conflicts it could split the band) and there are always family hassles about who's getting the limelight. Don't sign a long-term management contract with an inexperienced manager but remember you'll have to repay any investment he makes when you part from him and sign with another manager (hopefully at the same time as getting an advance for a recording deal).

If you pluck up the courage to advertise you'll get some replies. It is always hard for those without money to believe that there are people fumbling around trying to find somewhere to put their money, but it is a reality. It might as well come your way.

TRUSTING THE ENGINEER

Once you've got the money from one source or another and you've arranged the numbers to record in demo style (don't bother with more than two) you're ready to think about going into the studio.

Assuming you're not going to buy or hire the gear and record yourselves, you will end up relying on someone else — the sound engineer — to twiddle the knobs. He can have a make-or-break effect on how your demo sounds. You know in your head how your sound should be, but communicating that to some moron who's just recorded 25 cat-food jingles may not be too easy.

You are bound to end up taking pot luck over the choice of engineers, but if you're really calculating about your career, you should actually call into the studio you intend booking rather than phoning, and, while chatting to the person at reception you should ask to meet the engineer who would take your session.

You'll have two or three sentences in which to sum him up (it's invariably a man). If you can't stand the sight of him, or he seems to think you are beneath him, change your mind about the studio booking, make your excuses and leave. If you think he might be a nice bloke, take your chance.

WHO'S THE PRODUCER?

Before you go into the studio, work out who's going to produce the demo. It's probable that none of you will have had any production experience and, youthful democracy at work, you will probably agree that you'll all produce it. Remember: a camel is a horse designed by a committee and committee productions aren't much better. They give everybody the hump.

If there's someone in your group who has definite views about how the demo should sound, see if there is a consensus of agreement within the band for his or her ideas. You'll never get everybody to agree to anything that is individual, but if most members agree that on the whole one person's approach is right, follow that lead.

Professional production consists of two things: knowing what you want and then knowing how to get it in the studio. In your case, you only have the former talent, but it is most important that you do enter the studio knowing what you want. If you don't, you'll end up with a demo which doesn't only fail to sell you, but which doesn't even do you justice.

In rehearsal for the session, allow the person (or people) acting as producer to 'routine' you, as though they really were professional producers. This will pay off in the studio as everybody will know precisely what is expected of them. If the member who's producing plays an instrument which can be dubbed on after everything else is finished, allow him to stay in the control room and listen to everything as it goes down, telling the engineer roughly what is wanted.

To some extent you'll have to trust your engineer to interpret your ideas, since it is doubtful whether you'll have enough experience to operate the studio control desk successfully. If you can mix, and have had some experience at using items like limiters, echo chambers, digital delays, etc, don't hesitate to request control of the desk. Even if the engineer is a sticky sod who insists on hanging onto the chair, you move all the knobs and faders as *you* want and ask him not to interfere unless you're doing something that will mess the recording up. Remember that you are paying for the session!

Every band entering a studio for the first time is naturally nervous, so it's hard to remember that you're a paying customer who can insist on getting what you want. The most pathetic sight is to watch a new band sucking up to an experienced engineer in the hope that some crumb of praise about their music will fall from his lips: *forget it!* Any compliments he does pass about your music, and any enthusiasm he shows, is strictly in the line of business. Sound engineers do not listen in the way you do. Their ears are shot within a few months of working in a studio working with mediocre music for twelve hours a day. They may be able to hear technical things in sound (that's what they're trained for) but they are the worst judges of music in the world: they haven't got any listening space left inside their heads. So forget asking the engineer what he thinks of the track: you must be confident enough of your own music before you go in not to need false ego-boosting from a bored stranger. If he came up to you as a drunk after a gig you'd soon give him the push. Respond in the same way in the studio.

HIT TIP

If you've been using a roadie to do your sound-balancing while you've been on the road, it might not be a bad idea to give him the title 'associate producer' on the demo, so that he's encouraged to have a hand in the engineering. He's unlikely to know how to control the studio gear, and you may not think of him as the musical genius who's capable of producing your demo recording, but his experience at listening to you night after night and creating a balance in the echoing halls around the country will certainly help him to know whether the engineer is succeeding or failing to capture your sound on tape. He'll be at his most useful during the mixing stage — which can prove to be the most difficult.

MIXING

Mixing the final eight, sixteen or 24 tracks is probably the hardest of all tasks in any recording and this is particularly true for inexperienced bands. Being able to listen over and over again to the same track and create a growing and improving sense of balance between the individual elements of the song and instrumental lines is close to being an art form.

Occasionally a mix is arrived at easily: three takes and everybody agrees it's perfect. More often a mix is something that is worked at over many hours and, sometimes, over many days.

If you have a chance to use automated mixdown facilities, take it. It might be an idea to record the basic tracks at one studio and, providing the tape machinery is compatible, do your mixing at another which has computer-controlled mixing. Asking a computer program to take over the slog of remembering every move in a mix frees you for listening and judging — the creative part of mixing.

Don't allow every member in the band to have a hand in mixing: most musicians want to hear more of themselves than the rest of the band, they're only human. If it can be done tactfully, throw most of the band out of the studio while mixing. If it can't be done tactfully, throw them out anyway. You won't be able to mix in peace with six different opinions being aired.

HIT TIP

If your mix is proving difficult, wrap the session up and come back to it in a few days. Most mixes for master sessions are done separately to the main recording so that those concerned gain some sense of objectivity about the song. Ask for a rough mix of the session to take away on cassette. Listen to it endlessly the next day and then not at all for a week. The night before you're going back into the studio to make the final mix, listen to the rough mix once again and write down any notes you may have about what you want to do on the mix. Don't go on listening to your rough mix or you'll destroy the objectivity you've waited for. This process ought to allow you to go back into the studio and mix reasonably dispassionately and, even if you are forced to re-record some parts, better that than producing a demo which does not coax a record company executive out of his office to see you.

Allow the engineer to create his first mix without comment. As he 'gets his sounds up' you should not comment, even though you can't hear the top synth line, or even if the Linn Drum is missing altogether — many engineers deliberately refrain from pulling all the elements of a track together until the last moment. Wait until he swings round and says 'How's that?' with a pleased grin on his face before you start to judge the track. If you don't like the mix, go right back to individual tracks and get a sound on them that corresponds with the sound in your head. Remember that any self-respecting studio should be able to offer you a vast range of sound options from speeding-up tracks (without altering pitch) to using such devices as vocoders and ring modulators after the raw tracks have been laid.

Build up your track slowly, always listening to the part-mixes with an ear of censorship, checking that the feel you want has been captured. Compromises during mixing are death, if they're absolutely unavoidable, they should be worked out thoroughly. You may not have the talent for this type of mixing. It takes real concentration: if you find yourself flagging after two hours, take a break. If someone in the band seems to have the magical gift of listening intently to the same things over and over again, hand the job over to him, or use him as your ears during the period your mind demands you switch off.

HIT TIP

Don't drink or use other stimulants while you are mixing. Half a pint of lager is enough to make you lose your hearing above 16K and if you do try a mix when you've 'had a couple' (of anything), you won't be able to judge the overall sound balance properly. It's a sober and serious job.

Finally, remember you're making a demo. Put everything into the first 30 seconds and worry less about the rest of the song. Unless the first blast is right, you can forget all of the later effort.

CASSETTES, TAPES OR LACQUERS

There was a time when all demos used to be on discs. Demos were cut onto special metal records coated with a super-soft lacquer which allowed about 30 plays before it disintegrated. Today almost every demo is offered on cassette.

It is worth getting the studio to duplicate cassettes for you; it doesn't cost a great deal and ensures true duplication of sound. Don't try duplicating them at home on a domestic cassette deck as you'll be spoiling the sound quality you have paid for.

Stipulate that the cassettes should be of the ordinary ferrite type with Dolby Noise Reduction *on*. Not every producer chooses to have a chrome/metal tape deck, but every chrome deck has a ferrite facility and everyone uses Dolby sound reduction. The difference in high-end response available with chrome tape is irrelevant in a demo.

How many copies of the cassette you order depends upon how you're going to set about using the demo recording to get a management or record deal (see the next chapter). Always buy the master stereo *and* the master multi-track tape from the demo studio. Never leave such things behind. When you've had your hit you can be sure someone will try to use them against you if you've been neglectful. Getting a hit is a lot to do with attention to detail.

4

GETTING A RECORD DEAL

(**NOTE:** Bands usually find good management (or legal representation) only after they have the offer of a good record deal, but sometimes it is the management which secures the deal, in which case read Chapter 5 first).

This is probably the most important chapter in this book. Until the beginning of the 1980s, management was probably the most vital ingredient in a pop act's success, but today the pendulum has swung back in favour of the record companies and the quality of the record deal secured by an act is now the most important element on the road to making hit records.

THEY WANT YOU AS MUCH AS YOU WANT THEM!

Record companies are desperate for new acts. They have never been so desperate as they are today and the reason is simple: their industry, the one you have chosen to work in, is suffering from a declining market.

In the peak years of the fifties, sixties and early seventies the record business was booming. Each year saw sales exceed estimates and, despite a few years of temporary recession, most people involved felt growth was the natural way of all things musical. Now music no longer holds the central position in youth culture. It has been replaced by many diverse activities. Pop music has been an escape for youth for over fifty years, but the arrival of videos, computers, electronic games and easy-to-get recreational drugs, has toppled pop from its premier position as the opiate of the people.

The result is that fewer and fewer records are sold: there are still some giant successes, of course, but the boardroom reality is that fewer young people are choosing to spend their disposable income on pre-recorded music. Growth has been nil, with figures between 1978 and 1983 showing a downturn each year in real terms. Profitability, the all-important barometer of any business, has also been severely hit. In the mid-1970s the UK record industry generated pre-tax profits which ran at about twelve to fourteen per cent of turnover. By 1979 this had been completely eroded and in 1980 the average figure was a two per cent loss on turnover. In the last few years profits have begun to climb again — to approximately eight per cent before tax — but this is still well down on the profit level needed for a healthy trading position. The lift seen in British recordings from 1983 onwards has almost entirely been due to the impact that British music has made in the American market as a result of British dominance of the cable TV station, MTV.

The music business has become a 'fashion' industry with fewer artists selling more records in shorter spaces of time. The market profile of a recording act is now more like a culture craze such as hulahoops, skateboards or Rubic cubes than the type of ten or twenty year career that was enjoyed by artists who rose to prominence in the 1960s. Fashions have a rapid turnover which is why record companies are desperately seeking new acts. Even when a label has a couple of million-seller artists on their books, the company knows that the artists are unlikely to have a long life. For this reason they have to discover and invest in new acts as quickly as possible. The pop music business has become much more 'instant' and the result is that record companies are having to work harder to maintain their profitability.

This can result in quite amazing deals being offered to new bands who look as though they represent or lead a new trend. Advances of £200,000 are now not uncommon for new acts, but record companies are being more careful about how they describe advances. Formerly they were almost always un-recoverable: the only way for a record company to get its money back was to sell lots of records and withhold the artists' royalties until the advance had been paid. Now words like 'redeemable' and 'recoverable' are entering into record company contracts which now lay some responsibility on the act to be successful.

TAPING AND THE PIRATES

Record sales are also declining globally for reasons other than a change in the mood of youth culture. Cassette tapes have had an appalling effect on the international record business. For every one record sold, the industry estimates that four are taped from radio plays. Losses to the British recording industry are currently estimated as being over £1,000 million a year and in a 1984 survey 41 per cent of the British adult population admitted to carrying out some form of home taping. This wasn't happening in the fifties and sixties and, in the album-dominated early seventies, wasn't practicable.

HIT TIP

A special Joint Anti-Piracy Intelligence Group, JAPIG, has been formed by the IFPI (International Federation of Phonographic Industries) and the International Chamber of Commerce's International Maritime Bureau. The group is run by a lawyer who works with the Commonwealth Crime Unit to combat tape piracy.

Another major problem has been the alarming rise in counterfeiting. A record which is successful in the UK or the USA is almost certain to be successful in overseas markets. In years past the overseas branches of the major labels have been charged with the job of getting the record into the Top Ten in Brazil, or India, or Chile, Argentina, or whatever. Now their main job is to hunt the pirates. The moment a record is successful in either of the main markets, the pirates have got a duplicate of the master tape (average bribe to a studio engineer £1,000) and after printing records with lookalike labels they are sold via highly-organized distribution channels to normal record outlets across the third world.

HIT TIP

The industry is so concerned about the emergence of home taping that they have been bringing pressure to bear on hardware manufacturers who seem to be producing equipment specifically designed to facilitate such copying. For instance, in 1984 Aiwa agreed to discontinue distribution of its double-headed high-speed cassette machines in Britain after representations were made to the company by the record companies' trade association, the BPI.

Most record companies want to see a levy put on the price of blank tapes which would be shared out among record companies pro rata against the popularity of their product, and the British government now also seems convinced that this is the correct way to deal with the problem of home taping.

The EEC Commission, however, seems to be looking favourably on the idea that there should be a levy to offset the losses which are currently being suffered by the record companies. Levies are already in force in Sweden and Norway and this has seemingly led to a reduction in sales of blank tapes – although a corresponding increase in pre-recorded tapes and records is not yet apparent.

Artists, songwriters, publishers and record companies don't see a cent, a rouble, a pfennig or a drachma from these pirated releases: all they get is complaints if any of the pirated records or cassette tapes are faulty. The problem is much bigger than record companies are currently admitting. They fear that owning up to the fact that three-quarters of the world-wide potential of a hit recording will go to organized crime will be enough to put major managers off offering new acts to them.

No one can say precisely how much is lost in this way, that figure is obscured by the nature of the fraud. But it must be pointed out that all information (and music can be included under this heading) is now becoming available for endless and cheap copying and there may have to be a major shift in western society's values about the perceived notion of 'ownership' in a work of art or a piece of information to accommodate the computer age. Many socialists wonder why a songwriter should get paid over and over for one piece of work while a car worker only gets paid once. It's an unanswerable political question, but when a songwriter can spend twenty minutes producing one song which pays him enough so that he never has to work again, the point is clearly made.

HIT TIP

Pirates and counterfeiters don't only operate in the third world; several UK operations have also been uncovered by the police and the BPI. Typical of these is the case of ex-Edison Lighthouse member David Tewes. After failing to repeat the giant 1970 hit *Love Grows Where My Rosemary Goes* (which was very much a studio production by the song's writers Tony Macauly and Barry Mason), Tewes and partners set up a company which produced more than 500,000 pirate audio cassettes in fifteen months. Tewes and his partners admitted the piracy to the High Court in 1984 and said they had been producing 10,000 counterfeit tapes a week.

HIT TIP

It has been suggested that another reason for declining record sales in Britain has been the re-emergence of radio. After their mid-sixties heyday, radio pirates were fairly quiet until 1983, when they burst back on the music scene with a vengeance. In mid-1984 no fewer than 31 pirates were operating in the UK according to government figures. Most successful of the new pirates has been Radio Laser (558 metres, medium wave) which plays almost non-stop chart music. The problem is that Laser and the other pirates pay no fees for the records they play and don't observe any needle-time agreements with the Musicians' Union. As a result, the listening public is offered a constant diet of non-stop, uninterrupted chart music for which musicians and record companies receive no payment. Despite this, it has become clear that some record companies and promoters have been supplying Laser and other pirates with free records and have even been trying to canvass air play. Such activity is an offence under the Marine, &c., Broadcasting (Offences) Act 1967 and, more importantly, clearly injurious to the long-term health of the record industry. But the lure of securing the short-term success of a record as a hit often outweighs all such considerations.

For all of these reasons, the record business is not a good one for heavyweight business investors. Don't think that there are no investors, however, for they're queueing to get in. The sort of investor with a million or two is still heavily attracted to the music business because profits from individual projects can still be high, but the corporate investors are staying away from recorded art and are investing in the media which are reducing recorded art's long-term profitability, e.g. computers and new technology products.

As record sales decline overall, so record companies get more desperate for *the new*. It is this that sells so, increasingly, the accent is on novelty. The music business was always about new things and new ideas, but now the concept has become an obsession and record producers are scrambling over themselves in a frantic attempt to find the act that will keep them up in a diminishing market.

You're probably in the music business because you have no choice — it's the thing you do best. But you should know that you're entering an industry that is already beginning to slip into yesterday.

SENDING OUT THE DEMOS

The traditional method of getting a record company or a major producer interested in your act is to send out copies of your demo tape to them and then hope to receive an instant call to the record company offices. It almost never happens that way. Why?

There are lots of reasons: the first is that your music will be heard under the coldest of conditions (but remember, it always gets heard). Nobody in the record company knows you, nobody has got any feeling about your tape other than a usually justified feeling of pessimism about all the unsolicited tapes that arrive at record company offices.

Book publishers call the unsolicited manuscripts that pour into their offices the 'slush pile' and although they read every manuscript (or, at least, part of every manuscript) they generally regard such offerings with disdain. If, however, a manuscript arrives by hand from one of the most powerful literary agents in London then it is read carefully, with some warmth in the spirit of the reader. If the manuscript receives a poor report from the first reader in the publishing company, a senior editor is likely also to read part of it to ensure the house is not missing something of importance. They know the agent and they doubt that he would be wasting their time on something hopeless.

It is just the same in the record business. It is all those hopeless housewives, bus drivers, teachers and gas board clerks who send in tapes of their singing budgerigars that spoil your chances. Record companies use a much nastier word than 'slush' about the material that drops unasked for through their letterboxes.

It is for this reason that you should think seriously about trying to get someone from the record company to see your live act before you submit a demo. Another alternative is to get a manager, or well-known music business lawyer, before you go for a record deal (see next chapter). A manager who already has two internationally-known acts is going to receive respect when he rings the chief executive of EMI and tells him that he's sending over a tape he really must listen to. But, like the chicken and the egg, you may have to try for the record deal before you attract any influential manager or lawyer and cast off the thousands of would-be managers who only claim to have influence.

Another reason why sending out a demo rarely succeeds in getting a deal for a band, is that the task is hardly ever undertaken in a professional and thorough way. The rules are quite simple, but they are almost never followed.

You may have prejudices about certain record labels, but you need to examine the charts for the past two years and throw away your instinctive feelings. Work out which are the labels with consistent success – you'll find that there's a list of about 30. If you visit your local library and go through all the old copies of *Music Week*, the music industry's trade paper, you'll also find the names of the producers of each hit. If necessary, develop a card index for each name or label you find in the charts and enter their score every time you come across another hit bearing the same credit. Very quickly you'll end up with a clear idea about who dominates the charts and with what sort of act. (You should also look at Bert Muirhead's *The Record Producers File*, Blandford Press, 1984).

You should end up with a list of about 50 names and addresses which will include the major record companies such as EMI, CBS, Warner Brothers, etc, the smaller independent labels which are successful, and record producers' names. (A list of record company addresses appears in the appendices to this book).

HIT TIP

It is well worth examining which labels are the most successful in the charts. *Music Week* regularly include diagrams which shows the breakdown of UK single and album sales company by company. Those for the first part of 1984 are unlikely to change significantly over the next few years.

The one element which has changed in this decade is that the 'other labels' are now taking a wopping 32.6 per cent of the singles market and 48.8 per cent — nearly half — of the album market.

For this reason it is not possible to say that one label is necessarily better than another in terms of making individual hits, although the graph makes it clear that CBS, EMI, Virgin, RCA, WEA, Phonogram and Polydor all consistently make hits.

It is difficult to develop a good list of record producers' addresses. After you have developed a list of the most successful producers, visit your local Head Post Office and look up the names in the London telephone directory. Many producers name their companies after themselves and you'll fill in a few blanks this way. When you've exhausted this avenue, ring the record companies on which their product is released and ask for the producer's office address: you will usually be answered courteously and given the information.

If you become desperate and can't get information on a few names, ring *Music Week* (01-836 1522) and ask for the editorial department.

Whatever you do, complete the mailing list. If you don't you'll never know whether the name you missed off might have been the person prepared to make you a hit.

HIT TIP

It's worth seeing if you can get access to a word processor. Many schools, colleges and offices now have word processing power and even if you don't know how to use a computer, you may be able to persuade someone to put your mailing list on for you. It is also worth asking a word processing bureau for a quote for writing 50 letters: it's unlikely to be much more than £40.

The advantage of using a word processor in this way is that each person or company to whom you are sending your demo will receive a fully personal letter, yet the 50 letters can be run out automatically in about an hour. If you have to sit down and type 50 individual letters, the chances are it won't get done.

Also, having the addresses stored in computer memory offers you easy access to check who's responded and who hasn't. You'll certainly have to chase some of them up.

THE ACCOMPANYING LETTER

There's no need to say very much in the letter you send out with your demo cassette. Keep it short and simple, but ensure that it offers enough detail. Here is a sample:

Dear (Record Producer)*,

I enclose a demo cassette of my band, Lost Youth. All of the material on the tape is our own — we recorded it at XYZ Studios last month.

We're five piece — keyboards, guitar, drums/percussion/programmed percussion, bass and lead vocals — and we've been working together for a year.

We play live three or four times a month and if you'd like to see us live, I'm sure we can arrange a gig near London for you.

Thanks for your interest.

Yours sincerely,

*Insert his name.

The last paragraph only applies if your band does take on live gigs. If you're planning to start out as a studio band you can just delete it. The claim about being able to fix a gig near London should be made even if you've no idea about how you could do it. The lesson to be learned is: stick your neck out and risk it. If a major producer does tell you he'd like to see your live act, you'll find a way of playing in London.

It is now not done to include still photographs with your demo. A few years ago the obligatory studio shots always showed a bunch of self-conscious musos in a limp pose, but today it has got to be a video or nothing.

IS A DEMO VIDEO WORTH IT?

Yes. If you can find the money to put a reasonable quality video of your act together, do so. It is by far the best way to sell yourself. But there are many problems in making a demo video, the greatest of which is the high cost.

Don't consider trying to make an 'art' video in which you loon about intercutting with shots of Nazi marchers or similar 'directed' effects. If you perform live, tape one (or several) of your concerts and edit from that.

Using a local video production house, two cameras and a day's editing, it's going to cost you about £2,000 to make a five minute video. You'll also have to raise the money to make a high-quality sound recording of the gigs and marry that together during the dubbing and editing stage. This will cost a further £1,000 or so unless you have your own studio system.

If you know you're good, it's money well spent. If your act is particularly visual, then you really ought to strive to find the money for a video. Videos arriving at producers' offices are still much rarer than demo tapes and always get looked at with greater interest: the mere fact that the demo is on video indicates how serious you are about your career.

HIT TIP

WARNING: The video is a much crueller medium than the recording tape. If you look naff, or your act looks naff, it can be seen in seconds! Don't make a video unless you're absolutely sure that the way you look and perform on stage is both fresh, interesting and, most importantly, non-derivative.

Don't allow anyone from the video production house to try and do a Fellini on you. Over-weird shots and moody lighting are OK if they don't get in the way of your act, but the first thing you must demand of the director is that he shows the band in the clearest possible light. You will all be tempted to turn the video into a production which shows what clever video makers you all are: *don't*. The object is not to sell your video-making abilities (although they may be useful later) but to showcase your band. Clever direction will get in the way.

When Trevor Horn, or any other successful producer, puts your tape on his VHS machine and sits back to watch, he'll be listening to the music, looking at the people and then looking at the way they appear together on the stage. These are the priorities.

Try and use a small packed club in which to make the demo. Paper the hall liberally with friends and ask them to do their best for you out front. Don't worry too much about how you play that night, but worry more about how you look and the way you present the act. Play your numbers strictly according to the way you have rehearsed them: you'll later have to marry the video shots to a sound record so it is worthwhile taking mechanical time from a drum machine and trying to stay with it as much as you can. For a professional video you would normally mime to an existing track, but this won't get you the right atmosphere for an inexpensive demo video. If you think you're good enough, you can record your on-stage sound and use that as the demo, but the problem is that songs for a demo video have to be structured differently — like demo tapes — to songs intended for on-stage or master recording use.

If you want to be a studio band, a video won't be of much use to you. If you've got a couple of exceptionally good faces in the band consider falling back on the old idea of sticking a photograph in with the demo tape, but drop the idea of making a video unless money is no problem.

Send all demo videos out on VHS format cassettes. Nobody really uses any other format in the music business.

GETTING THE DEMOS OUT

The most important mantra word on your road to a hit is persistence. Having made a demo tape and/or video which you feel is good, you must persist in getting it heard in the right places.

The most natural human approach is to send copies to the top half dozen producers and, when the rejections arrive, give up dispiritedly and go back on the road for six months (or, sometimes, break up the band). This is lethal. You must plan to get a written rejection from every name on your carefully prepared list before you call the project a failure. If 49 out of the 50 have rejected your demo, it still has not failed! It only fails when *all* 50 have said no. Thinking any differently is to lose the chance of making a hit.

If a demo costs you £1,000, think of the project as costing you £20 to allow each producer to hear your band: that's a pretty good deal and you should not be content until every single producer has commented.

Although administration does not figure prominently in the life of a band, try to get someone to think in an organized way about sending demos out. Make it one person's sole responsibility and, if you have a relative, or friend, willing to take on the task, hand it over. They'll do it much more objectively than you will. Also, they'll probably do it much more efficiently.

HIT TIP

Expect to be rejected. Remember how many companies turned the Beatles down. The rejection may not be a comment on your talent, but a comment on the type of act the producer is looking for, the financial state of the label or any one of a thousand other elements. Out of the master list of 50 or so possible markets for your music, perhaps only five or six (and you won't know which ones they are) will be ready for you.

There is only one answer to the awful 'rejection blues' which set in each time a rejection arrives: the demo must go out again.

Make it a rule that each time a demo is returned, it is sent out again the same day. This is a psychological trick as it replaces the down feeling which follows a rejection with the glimmer of hope which rises when the demo goes out to a new label or producer.

How many copies of the demo tape you make will depend on how much you can afford. Try to get at least five made so that five copies are always out for consideration. Always enclose return postage (stick stamps to the bottom of your letter, don't bother with an envelope) but expect to lose two or three out of the five over the submission period.

Each submission will take between three and six weeks to turn round so, at an average of a month per submission, it will be clear that with five demo tapes it will take you ten months to reach all your possible 50 record companies and producers. If you have ten copies of the demo made, it will only take five months. It takes a long time to market a demo properly and in the meantime you should continue to work, to develop your act and to prepare for one of two options:

either to record some of the songs you have demoed in master form or to go in to record a new demo.

THE PERSONAL APPROACH

Although, sadly, it is true that it is *who* you know and not *what* you know which counts in this world, don't try and make personal contact by turning up at a record company or producer's door with your demo tape under your arm. All you'll meet is a stern doorman or a haughty secretary who will take out their own frustrations on you (because, secretly, they'd like to have your freedom). They'll put you down as hard as they can and you'll end up feeling like a worm. You certainly won't get to see the producer you had in mind.

HIT TIP

The exception to the rule of not telephoning producers is when you have lots of gigs in and around London (and it is worth trying your hardest to arrange them when you think you are ready to be seen).

Ringing a producer's office to ask him to come and see you is regarded as quite acceptable behaviour. At first, the secretary will take down the details of your gigs and politely tell you that the producer will do his best to get there (and each time you must leave his name on the door — never forget, it's so easy to wound the pride of someone who thinks he's important in the business; producers never expect to pay to get in); but if he doesn't show up at any of the gigs, you are definitely allowed to telephone again a few weeks later and leave another set of dates.

If you keep telephoning (and you remain polite) he will almost certainly come and see you.

This is a most important lesson that cannot be over-stressed: if you persist enough, you will get what you want.

If you know anybody who knows anybody, take advantage of this contact. Try to set up a meeting in a pub or club and, even if it means travelling a long distance just for the chance of a casual five minute meeting with the producer in a social situation, take the chance. If the producer likes you, he'll be warm to the demo when he puts it on. Like everyone else in life, producers like to like the people they already know.

Don't try telephoning record producers you've never met: you'll get an on-line put down only slightly less offensive than being kicked out of a record company reception area.

PERFORMING FOR A TALENT SCOUT OR A PRODUCER

The term 'talent scout' is very old fashioned and a few years ago it would have been laughed at, but it's come back into fashion with a vengeance as managers and producers increase their drive to find exciting new acts.

Junior office boys in management office and juniors in production offices do the circuit of London clubs freeloading at every venue and playing the Big-Time Music Business Person with the lowly bands they deign to talk to after the gig. Suffer these morons with a smile — they could be the key to getting a major producer or manager along to hear you. Don't give these obnoxious young idiots the treatment they deserve.

It hardly needs saying that when you're playing in areas where you may be seen by scouts (such as the inner London clubs) you need to be performing at top form. Although it goes against all of the best showbusiness tradition of the show going on, and all that, don't perform at a sensitive venue if you're not at full strength or if your gear isn't working properly. It is better to miss a gig than to be seen by a scout (or worse, a major producer) when you're not on top form. Once you've been seen and rejected by a producer you'll find it almost impossible to get him to see you again, so better not to turn up at the gig than turn up without your synth player and produce a dreadful sound which will make him turn round and go on to the next club after half a number.

GOING TO LONDON

It will have become clear from the foregoing that London clubs are important venues. A few of the more dedicated management offices do send scouts out into the provinces, but most believe (rightly) that they are so powerful the talent must come to them.

You should consider moving to London (even on a temporary basis) if you live and are playing in the provinces. There are some exceptions: each major city, such as Glasgow, Edinburgh, Liverpool, Bristol, etc, has its own music scene and these are visited fairly regularly by producers on the nose round for new talent, but you must ask yourself whether you wish to be seen as 'a band from Newcastle' or whether you would prefer the anonymity of being a great-sounding band in a London club.

It is very hard to move to London if you're from the provinces. Accommodation is almost impossible, work is hard to find for bands (although it is hard to find everywhere) and you'll be sticking your neck out in a very big way. But it still seems to be worth it. Sleeping on other people's floors, putting up with nasty landlords, the occasional night in the back of a car, pale beside the opportunity afforded to musicians and bands who play the London clubs regularly.

Don't expect to earn a living from playing clubs in the capital. They all know how valuable their location is and the desultory and insulting money they offer bands effectively means you're paying for the privilege of playing to their bored and apathetic audiences (that's how you'll find many of them after provincial audiences) but if you're serious about making a hit you have to be seen by the right people. When the Beatles made their first record they were already folk heroes in Liverpool. It meant nothing in London. It had no influence on their first recording contract and many of the idiots in the record company which signed them would have been hard placed to find Liverpool on a map, let alone travel there to hear a new band. It's a sad but inescapable fact of life, that the action which matters is in London and you've got to go there if you want some of it.

THE DEAL

Let's make a major leap of imagination and assume that you've sent out your demos, a major producer or label executive has been interested enough to come and see you and he's been impressed by what he's seen.

The usual sequence of events which follows is a brief but awe-inspiring meeting in the sweat-box which serves as a dressing room after the gig at which the producer, usually humbly, says who he is and gives you his card with an invitation to come up to his office for a chat. He's likely to disappear almost immediately he's handed the card over and you, quite rightly, will party the night away in the knowledge that you're at least on the right road.

Don't hesitate about telephoning: ring at 11am the next morning. His secretary will fix an appointment for the following week and you'll ring off feeling ten miles tall. This will be one of the best moments of your career: no matter how many platinum or gold discs you receive after this, this first acknowledgement by the professional music business will give you a high which may never be equalled, except perhaps by your first Number One hit.

It's not a good idea for the entire band to turn up at the meeting with the producer or label, although it is understandable that everybody will want to. If you risk a total upset within the band, then take everybody along, but it is kinder to the producer and it will lead to a more relaxed and honest meeting if only two of you go, and these two should include the front man (or woman) and the major songwriter.

The only reason a producer or label executive will ask to see you is that he is considering recording you. He won't be making the invitation to pass on friendly tips, or to give you other non-involved encouragement: he'll be looking for a deal.

Be ready for some shocks at this meeting. The producer may have completely different ideas about your band than you have. He might love the act exactly as it stands, but he might also want to alter some fundamental elements of it.

At the worst he might want to jettison some members of the band (and it could be you!) or he might want to alter completely the image and approach. At this stage you have to judge what he says by his track record. If you've been lazy and not done the chart research in *Music Week* recommended earlier you'll have to be non-committal at the meeting and ask for time to think the proposals over. If you know that he's been responsible for a string of major hits, or that the label is powerful, you should give careful consideration to his suggestions. If the offer comes directly from a successful producer, you will know he's found the hit formula and, what's even more important, the rest of the industry know he's found it and accord his new productions semi-hit status the moment they're released. This is vital.

You may be faced by a major moral dilemma: if the producer or label wants you to fire your bass player who's also your closest friend, you have to choose between stamping on your friend's face on the way up the ladder (and earning his life long emnity) or turning your back on success.

No one can provide you with the answer to this problem, but my personal experience after many years in the music business is that those who make the hard decision and stamp on their friends are the ones who succeed and those who take the morally correct decision are the ones who never make it. Life is not fair.

Another consideration is that those who make the 'right' moral decision may end up, years later, bitterly regretting their loyalty. If success never comes, they'll be left with the feeling 'if only . . . ' and this can be a gut-rotting bitterness which erodes the friendship they sacrificed their chance for. It's a personal decision always, but if a hit matters to you more than anything else, you know what the decision should be. If you think this way, you should also be prepared to be dumped in your turn later in your career: be sure that it will happen.

CREATING AN AUCTION

Once you have one major producer or record company interested in your act, you should let the other record companies with whom you have been in contact know. Very often, several offers come together, or the news that one major label is interested serves to make the others look at the act again.

Let the other labels know before you get too involved with the person who first showed interest in you or you risk compromising his interest.

The situation you want to develop is one in which several labels are fighting for your signature on a contract. This is the way to produce six figure advances; it usually results in hit records being made.

There will be endless discussions with interested producers or record companies about image, recording, touring, management (if you don't already have it), and all the detail involved in turning a semi-unknown act into a nationally-known attraction. This differs in every case; what won't differ is that when you sign your recording contract, you should expect to receive an advance on your record royalties. How much this should be is a crucial step on the way to becoming a hit act.

THE ADVANCE

At this stage, the chronological progression from being an unknown act to a major chart band becomes blurred. You really need a heavyweight lawyer or manager working for you before the recording deal is finalized, but quite a few bands have been able to tie up wonderful record deals and then take their pick of the top managers or solicitors. It depends very much where you are in the business.

The advance will be paid by the record label, which will have the distribution rights to your 'product'. Even if you're initially signing with an independent producer, it is more common for the advance to come from the major company which makes and distributes the records than from the production house itself. There are exceptions and some producers are rich enough to pay huge royalty advances and so strike a better deal for themselves with the distributor. *Get as much in Advance as you can!* If you think this advice is stupid, or too obvious for words, think a little more about what a large advance means. Obviously, you would like to get £250,000 to share between you (ideally, according to the pre-written agreement of split percentages). You've put in the slog; the years of having no money when your working mates have had holidays and cars, the hard decisions you've had to make along the road and the debt which has piled up behind you and now which can be mercifully repaid.

But a large advance must be wrung out of a record company for another reason: it is the only thing which *guarantees* that your single will be treated as 'priority' when it comes out. We met the word 'priority' in Chapter 1; it really means everything in today's business. If your record is a priority product you'll have a hit: if it's not, you won't.

Taking an advance so large that it hurts the record company, forces them to make your product priority just to ensure they get their money back. The question that will now be in your mind is 'how do you force them to pay a huge advance?'

The size of advance paid by a record label depends on three things:

1 The track record and power of your producer (if he's yet appointed).
2 The track record and power of your manager or lawyer.
3 The collective opinion of your talent within the record label.

Your talent and ability is a definite 'third' on that list. If your lawyer is Alexis Grower and you're going to be produced by Trevor Horn, you can be fairly sure of a six figure advance. There are a dozen other combinations of producer/manager which will also push you into that league. It is still worth going with the deal if you're in the second league, so long as both your producer and manager are hit makers.

If you're offered a small advance on a record deal, with an 'up and coming' producer and a new manager, or a manager who hasn't had a hit act for some years: don't take it! Do you have the strength to resist? After years in the cold someone's beckoning you into the warmth: it's very hard to say no, but say no you must if you want to be *sure* of making a hit.

Remember that you are likely to be ripped off when you become a star. Some comments in this book should help you to accept that fact deal with it sensibly rather than in a way which is going to wreck your career. If you think in this way you will find it easier to resist the lure of the small-time deal. Today's record business has changed to such an extent that only the very luckiest of the small managers and producers can crash through the cartel now operated by the big companies and if you're not with the big boys, your recorded music just won't be heard by the British and international public.

CHRONOLOGY OF THE DEAL

Assuming that you are able to get several record labels interested in you at the same time, you need to get yourself an expert manager or lawyer to negotiate the deal for you. A manager will charge around fifteen to twenty per cent of your gross earnings for this privilege, a lawyer will charge you hefty fees. (British solicitors aren't allowed to take percentages).

Your choice of a lawyer or manager depends on your own ability at handling business. The less you know the more you need a manager, the more you know the more a solicitor becomes the right adviser.

Any record company hoping to sign you will insist on you consulting your own lawyer at the point of signing a contract, to protect themselves from possible future accusations that you signed a deal without proper independent advice. In any case, any manager you hire will, in turn, bring in a lawyer to go over the contract.

Whichever type of negotiator you appoint, he will start dictating terms to the interested record companies. It is at this point that your future hangs in the balance. The ability to dangle several companies on a string while establishing the fact that you are a 'hot' band is vital. If you or your negotiator succeeds, you will be able to run an 'auction', a day when companies are invited to bid against each other for your services.

A contract auction isn't normally a 'Dutch' auction — few companies will bid unless they know who the competition is, but an auction is the sure way of pushing up your advance until it reaches the critical stage and assures that every effort will be made to turn you into a hit act.

PAYMENT OF THE ADVANCE

If you get an advance over £100,000 it might be wise not to take it all at once. Understandably, young people who've never had any money aren't likely to welcome accountant-type caution even before they've bought their first new car, but it's this sort of attitude which makes the young pop star such a wonderful golden-goose. He becomes a very vulnerable target for the rip-off.

If you're really cool, get some instant heavyweight accountancy advice about getting the money paid in the best way to avoid tax: if you've hired a lawyer rather than a manager he will almost certainly advise you to seek the advice of a tax specialist.

It is important that you understand the big difference between 'avoiding' and 'evading' tax. It is legal to avoid tax but illegal to evade it: often, avoiding it seems very much like evading it, but the accountants you will be paying have the responsibility of ensuring that you stay within the law.

If you do take the money all at once, and you've a substantial sum left over which isn't required for promotional purposes (more about how your money will be taken off you for such things in a later chapter), buy a house or a flat — even if you don't want one. Don't buy a new car, or take a month's holiday on the other side of the world until you have bought property. It is possible that you may never see a lump sum such as that again, so use your first real money as though it were going to be your last, and turn it into a substantial asset.

THE CONTRACT

There is no standard contract between recording artist, producer and record label. Basically, it will say that in return for the money and a promise to make and release records, you will only make a specific number of records for the company. The typical deal specifies four albums. This type of deal is written in a thousand different ways and very often qualifications are put on both parties: how many records will be released over what period, how much promotion the record company will do, how many tracks the band will record, etc.

This book should be no substitute for an experienced music business lawyer's advice, but the normal term of contract (when a number of tracks is not stipulated) is five years and a 'good' percentage for a new act signing a record deal is between eight and ten per cent of the retail price of the record. (Remember that you are likely to have to give away several per cent — perhaps as many as four out of your ten — to producers, promoters and managers. Also remember that the ten per cent of an album's selling price, perhaps 60p out of £6, often has to be split four or five ways in a band).

There are a thousand other details which need to be examined; overseas rights and the royalty paid in these territories being probably the most important. Seek experienced advice on these matters, but there is one important principle you should understand: you are likely to be ripped off in the first two years. An increasing number of young bands are managing to avoid making it a catastrophe, but old music business lore makes it clear that there is almost no way to avoid it if you wish to become a star. This fact of life is explored in more detail in the following chapter on management, but the principle is so important that you should think in the right way when considering a record deal. If you reveal yourself to be such a smart operator that you spot all of the nasty clauses in the recording contract and you, and your lawyer, iron out every twist and bend that is in the producer's and record company's favour, you run the serious risk of having the offer cancelled.

Handled in the right way, the smart artist can protect himself from the worst excesses of exploitation, but in general the aim of nearly all producers and record companies is to extract huge sums of money from people they turn into stars. If the people they select for this honour reveal themselves to be faster and more competent in business at the start of the game, many producers and labels prefer to ignore any talent the individual may have and switch their efforts to someone else who they feel they can manipulate more easily. This is why the lawyer you hire to negotiate your record deal must be experienced: he will have learned how to tie up a deal to your best advantage, while still leaving the moguls their pound of flesh. A lawyer who is not experienced in the music business will be likely to wind you up about the unfairness of the contract and could persuade you to reveal your hand far too early, or to blow your chances by misunderstanding the nature of the business and pressing for a contract which is too one-sided in your favour.

Apart from paying you the advance money, you shouldn't expect to see much in the way of other guarantees from record labels. Only very rarely will a contract stipulate the amount of promotion and advertising that goes behind a record and contracts never force record labels to release products at all. This is why a large advance is a vital necessity: it makes all such guarantees irrelevant. If the company has been made to pay an advance which hurts you can be sure they will throw in all the promotion necessary to recoup your money. It is the best guarantee of all.

5

DO YOU NEED A MANAGER?

There is a growing trend for pop acts to dispense with traditional management; it is certainly possible for you to manage yourself if you understand enough about business and if you're in a strong position — either with a good record deal or firm offers.

Several major bands have emerged since 1980 who have handled their own careers, but as managers now take fewer percentage points than they used to in the old days, you might be cutting yourself off from very valuable help (described later in this chapter) if you decide to go it alone.

It is also true that if you manage yourselves there will not be a manager who can steal money from you or otherwise cheat you. On the other hand John Lennon made it clear that Alan Klein would make a good manager for the Beatles even if they only got to see one million out of eight that they actually earned.

If you are going to manage yourselves you need excellent advice, an important new trend is for bands to employ lawyers and accountants on retainer and hand all the details over to them. Professional advisers can, of course, only respond to situations put to them: they are not in a position to seek out new opportunities, to mount TV spectaculars or to find new people for you to record with. A good manager is capable of doing all these things and if you don't have one, you'll inevitably end up with your own London office and have the headache of employing staff to run it.

USING A LAWYER

The American music business has been centred around lawyers for many years and the British industry is now following that example.

This has come about partly because of the greed and corruption of traditional pop music managers, who have cheated clients repeatedly and have given their profession its current bad reputation.

A solicitor is a professionally qualified person who is specifically debarred from any direct involvement with his client's money (other than under closely controlled circumstances) and although it is impossible to state that no lawyer will ever cheat you, it is highly unlikely, since to do so would almost certainly cost him his professional standing — something that he will have worked to achieve for many years.

Lawyers in the UK aren't allowed to take percentages from the acts they represent but an increasing number are fulfilling many of the duties of a traditional manager. Lawyers who specialize in the music business get to know all the record company chiefs, the producers and many of the artists. They join the business totally, going to the parties, staying on the yachts and even visiting recording sessions. For this reason their network of contacts is usually every bit as good as a manager's, but they usually have more respect in the business simply because of their professional standing.

Many bands are now starting to work closely with lawyers, often relying on them for many services not usually associated with legal skills. The negotiation of recording contracts is the obvious area in which a lawyer's skills are not only useful but vital, but lawyers are often involved in setting up tours and arranging TV and film contracts.

Lawyers also handle finance for bands, working closely with accountants who ensure that incoming money is used to their clients' best advantage. The combination of lawyer and accountant in this role is easily superior to that of a non-professional manager (who will still have to rely on lawyer and accountant) but it isn't right for every situation.

As you might expect, lawyers charge heavily for such services, but the principal advantage for a band is that the lawyer doesn't earn the right to fifteen per cent of your gross earnings for a set time. If the fee for the job is agreed in advance, or if the lawyer is working for an agreed monthly retainer, the band knows precisely what they will be paying and all other income is free from percentage take. Lawyers working in this way can become incredibly creative and the half-dozen best-known names in London are in huge demand from the stars.

Accountants tend to be of less use to the actual career of an artist or band. They are vital in the efficient handling of money, but whether the money has come from a Number One record or from a chain of launderettes doesn't alter the way in which they set about their task of conservation. It is the lawyer who becomes the band's chief adviser.

THINGS A MANAGER CAN DO

If you're bright, well educated (in the street sense, if not the literal), the foregoing section on lawyers and accountants might persuade you that you do not need a manager.

You may already run a successful, professional band which is able to command good fees and has a strong following. If this is the case, you are forgiven for wondering what it is any manager can do for you, but the right manager can transform a lack-lustre career into a brilliant performance and can open many doors which would otherwise remain closed.

You may use, and drop, managers at different stages in your career. The important thing is to avoid being bogged down by poor or mediocre management when your big chance comes along.

In general there are two types of manager: one type you should use and one type who will try to use you. The ideal, but very rare, situation is where you use each other.

THE 'TYPE 1' MANAGER

The first type was briefly discussed in Chapter 3. This manager will either be new to the music business or he'll be a 'has-been' manager who once managed one or two acts who had a brief spell in the limelight and who now desperately wants to fight his way back.

Do NOT sign a long-term agreement with either of these breeds of Type 1 manager. If possible, play them along, use their knowledge and help (and, if possible, their money) but do not be trapped into a contract.

Once upon a time it was normal for bands to be managed by a friend from their peer group who knew little more about the business than they did. It worked, briefly, in the 1960s, (Epstein, Loog Oldham, de Villeneuve, etc) but it can't work today; there's no room for ignorance. (Malcolm McLaren was the exception which proved the rule).

The Type 1 manager can supply you with one vital ingredient likely to be missing from the early stages of your career: money. Don't hesitate to take any that's offered, but don't sign anything that puts you into debt or which ties up your future freedom. Money is all the Type 1 manager has to offer you. Don't allow yourself to be captured by his personality: allow him his scenes of triumph (when he manages to get an important London club to book you), but always remember, you will have to switch managers on your way to a hit: 'they' (the establishment) won't let him (and in turn, you) in.

If money isn't a problem, don't waste your time with a Type 1 manager. (It need hardly be said that you shouldn't even talk to a Type 1 who hasn't got any money). Remember that if you take any investment money from a small-time manager you will have to pay it back, plus interest, when you have secured your record deal.

THE 'TYPE 2' MANAGER

The Type 2 manager is already rich and successful. He's got the international acts, he's got the money lifestyle of the houses, pools, yachts and international offices and *he holds the key to turning you into a hit act.*

No matter how experienced you are, how gifted a negotiator, how able a lawyer (you may even be qualified) how brilliant a hustler, you cannot open the right doors for your band unless you already belong to the inner circle of hit makers. (The type of lawyers mentioned earlier in this chapter are already fully initiated members of the circle).

Unless you already have the offer of a good recording deal, you need a Type 2 manager more than anything else: more than new instruments, more than new transport, even more than you need your own talent.

HOW TO GET THE RIGHT MANAGER

Successful managers will only sign you up for one thing: to make money out of you.

The standard management contract demands fifteen to twenty per cent from your gross earnings. In addition, if your manager is also your agent (as he invariably is today) you can say goodbye to a further ten per cent of gross earnings.

Being left with 65 per cent of your gross earnings may sound pretty good if, in return, you are to be hoisted from the obscurity of playing working mens' clubs to the heights of filling Wembley Stadium on a summer's evening. The fact is that unless you're very astute, you'll see very little of the money you make in the first couple of years of success.

You will only get the right manager if you're good and you're unusual. You need to have both elements in your act. The way to interest managers is to send a demo, but to follow it up with repeated calls to their office when you have gigs around London. This is one reason why living and working in London is so important. It is possible to make it straight from the provinces as several bands have demonstrated successfully in the last few years, but you will certainly improve your chances if you're available to be seen locally.

If you persistently, and politely, continue to request someone from a management office to see your act, someone will come, if only to stop your calls. Keep trying. You need top class management before you can achieve anything, but you should be aware of how dearly it is likely to cost you in the early years.

The operative phrase in management contracts is 'gross earnings'. Once you jump onto the merry-go-round of being a star, your perspective on earnings will go out of the window and your ability to judge gross against the much more important 'net' figure disappears. For this reason, you need to find a personal accountant who works for you, and only you, as soon as it seems likely you are going to secure a good advance. Bands can use one accountant working collectively for them, but after some chart success individual members must have their own personal advisers.

HIT TIP

The most important message in this book, and it is one I make no apology for stating over and over again, is that it is very likely that you will be profoundly ripped off on your way to the top. As it costs over £300,000 to put a single by a new artist into the British Top Five, no organization is going to put you there unless they see a massive return. This return can be won legitimately, by sharing in a massive success, but many managers (with the tacit approval of big record companies), help themselves to unearned slices of their artists' income just to make sure of the return.

Almost all would-be pop stars come from poor backgrounds and are broke during the period of their apprenticeship. None of their friends has money and they have no idea of what it is like to have sufficient money to bring dreams to life. For this reason they don't know how money works, they have no idea how to spend it properly or save it properly. Unless they are clever enough to appoint their own independent advisers, they rely entirely on advice from their managers and the accountants appointed by their managers, and that advice is likely to be suspect — at least when viewed from outside.

Not all successful managers are crooks — but a significantly high proportion could be described in this way. You may be lucky enough to be taken on by one of the managers who are totally fair and who will look after your interests as though they were their own, but the odds are against you.

The law of libel stops us from printing the names of the managers known to be crooks, but these names are well-known inside the music business. For a musician or band just starting out, it is very difficult to find out the truth about a manager or record company boss, especially when that person already manages very successful acts.

The only reasonable way to proceed is to assume that every manager is likely to rip you off until you discover otherwise. You must guard against paranoia, however, as extreme suspicion will often lose you an important contract. It is accurate to note that in many cases artists have to suffer being ripped off in order to make it. The best principal is to observe the general concept that the only person you can trust is yourself, but retain a pleasant outward attitude to the people with whom you are forced to do business.

HANDLING MONEY

The advance which follows the signature on a recording deal is likely to be the first 'real' money a musician sees. Much of this money will be spoken for and will go on re-paying long overdue debts, on buying the equipment the band has always needed and on gifts that the 'lucky' usually wish to give to family and friends. A month or so after the advance has been paid, most musicians discover that their bank balance only stands at a few thousand pounds.

This will still seem a lot to any musician who is used to owing the bank money or, more usually, being unable to find a bank which will tolerate his poor credit record. (Curiously, banks seem able to overlook such a record once an advance is paid).

The money from the advance can be seen as a light aperitif against the money that is generated from a Top Five single. As soon as the record enters the Top Thirty the money starts to flow: a professional manager will ensure that his band always has money in their pockets. Usually this money is provided as an 'advance' against what is coming in and what has yet to be distributed.

The system of the permanent 'advance' is one of the three principal methods used by less than scrupulous managers for keeping young pop stars under management control and in the dark about their own financial situation.

During my years in the music business I have seen a dozen world-famous bands kept satisfied by the 'advance' system and by another couple of methods discussed later. Each time a musician visits the management office his ego is stroked to the point of absurdity by the pretty and elegant staff members hired specifically for that purpose, and he always leaves his manager's office loaded down with more cash than he can spend in the next week or so (short of major purchases such as cars and houses which are always arranged 'through the office'). These weekly 'wages' are usually around £1,000 or £2,000 and the group members arc told to spend it, as rapidly as they can, since, they are often told, the principal aim is to reduce profit in the tax year to minimize the taxation burden. The pattern may differ from case to case, but the principal is the same: an effective smoke screen is being thrown up around the real financial situation and an insidious pattern is being created.

DRUGS

The second method of keeping stars 'tame' and malleable is by the use of drugs.

Most musicians use recreational drugs: marijuana, cocaine,

speed, general amphetamines and, sometimes, heroin. It is in the nature of the music business and if a musician chooses to avoid these drugs, he usually opts for another in the form of alcohol. The abstemious musician is a very rare animal.

Many managers double as drug dealers. They don't deal in the sense of being major wholesalers and they never 'sell' their goods, but they often become a source of constant supply for their artists. The most common drug used today is cocaine which has been popular in the music business for many years. I recall witnessing the weekly visits by an internationally-famous 'heavy' band in the early 1970s to an office just off London's Park Lane. Most of the band would come in on a Friday and each would collect two plastic bags. One contained cash — which they would sign for — and the other contained several grammes of cocaine, which they would not sign for.

Despite this 'service', managers are acutely aware of the dangers of losing their properties to hard drugs. They never offer heroin and they rely on the fact that 'dope and coke' are physically non-addictive (although they choose to ignore the occasional psychological dependence which follows prolonged use).

Few musicians are highly educated, although there is a sizeable minority with an IQ in the university league. All successful managers are sharp (by the process of natural selection) and don't find it too difficult to outmanoeuvre those who set themselves up as spokespeople.

During the peak periods of success, bands can be kept happy for months with a combination of ready cash, drugs, the natural ego food of becoming famous and, the last weapon in a manager's locker, sex.

SEX

All successful pop performers are offered endless easy sex; the unscrupulous manager's problem is to control this and use it to his own ends. One of the major headaches for a manager is when one of the star performers falls seriously in love, especially when the partner turns out to be a bright woman. The arrival of Yoko Ono and Linda Eastman on the Beatles' scene is an interesting and illuminating case well worth remembering.

For this reason, managers set out to wreck any dangerous romances they see developing, only feeling secure if the girl involved is likely to toe the line. They order road managers to procure the most beautiful girls possible for the star involved, and it is in the nature of young people that few are able to resist such temptation. There is no need for them to resort to prostitutes *per se*; the music business is filled with enthusiastic amateurs, but on several occasions on the road I have been aware that tour managers and others in the retinue have received special orders regarding one of the band members.

The heavy band referred to earlier caused their manager his biggest problem when a musician's wife (who he had inherited when he had signed the band) decided she'd like a swimming pool. For over two years the London office had been taking care of all financial needs. The band had been repeatedly told how rich they were becoming and they were reassured to learn that the money was being invested on their behalf in some very profitable companies. Everything went swimmingly, the cash, coke and girls formula keeping the members happy as sandboys week after week.

The problem occurred when the band were away on one of their bi-annual USA marathon tours. Sitting on the Midlands farm that the lead singer had bought with his earnings (actually, the office had bought it for him on his instructions) his bored wife, who usually accompanied him on all tours, got chatting to a neighbour who suggested they really ought to have a swimming pool. It made sense to the bored wife: after all, what was all the touring for if they couldn't have a pool when they wanted one?

Just as she had been told to do whenever she wanted anything, she called the management office to get it arranged. Somehow, the carefully arranged system for dealing with such enquiries broke down on this occasion as the manager had accompanied the band on the tour (presumably following the time-honoured Brian Epstein tradition of collecting all merchandizing percentages in cash on the night and depositing it under false names in small banks across America). The wife got no help: she was told to wait until the band arrived back in a month's time.

The wife — we'll call her Joy — decided that it would be great to give her hardworking husband a surprise by getting the pool put in before his return and she popped along to see her own bank manager to arrange a temporary loan for the money so she could get the work underway immediately. Her bank manager was delighted: he said there were no problems in providing the loan, all Joy would have to do was deposit the deeds to the farm with the bank as security during the period the money was being borrowed.

Two days later Joy was shopping in London — using her credit cards which were automatically paid for by 'the office' — and she decided to pop into HQ to collect the deeds necessary for the bank loan. She was greeted by one of the manager's assistants and, through a gross piece of inefficiency, she left with the deeds in her pocket ten minutes later.

The following day she handed them over to the bank and, after a few moments, was told that the deeds weren't in her name or her husband's. The farm was owned by a Swiss company.

The singer didn't get his pool. When he returned home Joy was able to present him with proof that things weren't as they had thought. It is said that the meeting between the singer and the manager which followed in the elegantly-furnished London office was violent in the extreme — certainly the manager was hospitalized and several items of antique furniture were smashed.

In the aftermath it was revealed that every major asset bought in the group's name turned out to be the property of a Swiss company owned by professional Swiss nominees (and thus it was impossible to trace who the real owners were) and when, on the eventual demand for the money owed to the band (they had finally brought in an independent auditor on their behalf) the request was countered with highly detailed and itemized counter-claims of un-paid advances and expenses that almost equalled the gigantic sum they had earned.

Three-year-old receipts for hamburgers for the road crew and similar items were all produced with a contemporary description of every expense prepared by one of the management staff. The result was a two-year legal battle which was finally settled out of court. The band got about twenty per cent of what they were originally told was due to them. Ten years later they have re-built their career (after a few years in the wilderness) and today have a manager who is primarlily an accountant, working for them.

There are many such stories in the music business, most of them true. Unlike other types of story, the stories about lost money are usually played down by the participants who hate being seen for the fools they are. A few of the cases have come into the open, however. It took Gilbert O'Sullivan years to get justice over his deal with manager Gordon Mills, but finally the High Court found in his favour and awarded him huge amounts of money. The judgement ruled that the manager had 'exploited and fleeced' Gilbert O'Sullivan and returned the songwriter's copyrights to his ownership. Most such disputes are kept secret.

In the late 1960s I managed a band in the West London area. They had a futuristic name and, besides playing exceptionally well, their lead guitarist was also very handsome. The band never got anywhere and it broke up a year or so later, but I was particularly pleased to see this guitarist shoot to national prominence in the mid-1970s when the band he had formed had three successive Number Ones and followed them by Top Ten albums in Britain, the States and the rest of the world.

Two years after his first hit I met him again, for the first time since his success. I was delighted for him and told him so.

'Would you believe I'm still living in the same bed-sit in Richmond?' he asked me, with a bitter smile. It had happened again. He had the fame, the name, the adulation, the girls (he didn't use drugs much), but he didn't have the money.

The traditional split between band and management occurred ('for personal reasons') and, after the short period of inactivity that seems to follow all such traumas, they are now back as an international headline act, currently one of the most successful live acts in the world.

The business is littered with stars and ex-stars who should have made enough money to support them for the rest of their lives but who are now broke. Many of them were foolish with their money, but nearly all of them suffered from being cheated by unscrupulous managers.

EXPENSES

Of all the jargon words in the world of accountancy and money, 'Xs' is the one which is most abused by the music business.

Imagine yourself with your first record climbing the charts. Although nothing inside you has changed, now your telephone doesn't stop ringing. Within a few days your diary is full for weeks ahead, then for months. Journalists keep wanting to interview you about your views on anything and everything and each time you are interviewed you're taken out to get your picture taken. This can happen ten times a day. Then it's television: first a few provincial shows, then, suddenly, 'Top of the Pops', the Saturday morning kids' shows, the late night shows. Everything is happening at such a pace, you don't know where you are. Finally, the ultimate happens. People stare at you in the streets, only instead of staring in interest, they're staring in recognition.

If you're playing live dates during this period, the audiences will suddenly switch from being indifferent to being wild about you. It's all a whirl and it is one of the best times of your life. You're on a massive high, and so you should be, but one thing is certain: you don't feel like spending four hours every day in an accountant's office studying the finances. You're being given massive amounts of cash, you have public adulation, you're always in front of the cameras and it's a bad day when you can't find at least one mention of your name in the popular press.

Your 'high' from this type of first success lasts, on average, about

Bronski Beat are fun, but do they have substance? This hasn't been a chart requirement in the last ten years, but if the band want to develop, they' ll have to show us more.

Trevor Horne (*left*) is probably the most successful British producer of the 1980s. From his first hit as performer and producer of *Video Killed the Radio Star* by Buggles he's gone on to huge successes with ABC, Dollar and, most recently and notably, FGTH. If anyone knows how today's business works, it's T. Horne. *(Ray Hammond)*

Big Country — a band that can play!!! There are still some bands who make it by working hard, even though the machinery still has to fly American journalists in on free junkets and ride the promo train.*(LFI Ltd.)*

Bananarama come across as a highly manufactured act, one which has been put together with cool calculation about the mood of the business. Despite some definite talent, the band will have to split or adapt to find long-term success. *(LFI Ltd.)*

Is there life after hype? Examine the career of Adam Ant for the answer. *(LFI Ltd.)*

Paul Young has a great voice and he's managed to get the hits without resorting to daft posing. There's a lot to be said for this and we should have high hopes for his future. *(LFI Ltd.)*

Having a great voice has been George's saving, certainly he wouldn't have survived this appalling image if he had been as talentless as his imitators. *(David Levine/Virgin)*

Simple Minds were one of the bands who broke through by combining great fashion sense with ability. There was a carefully created 'buzz' about them in the business long before they found public success. *(LFI Ltd.)*

Talent does come out these days despite the manipulations of the chart. Nik Kershaw's a great example, but he's still very much part of the hit process. *(LFI Ltd.)*

Duran Duran can be thought of as a 'cross over' act. They sell records to many people outside of the narrow teen band which exercises its influence on the charts. The band combines the late 1970s' synthesiser approach with the high fashion of today. *(LFI Ltd.)*

Howard Jones is another highly talented act who has currently allowed his abilities to be exploited inside the pop machine. His talent is apparent, but as yet his appeal is limited. *(LFI Ltd.)*

Steve Strange can take a lot of credit (or blame) for adding to the ephemerality of high fashion in the pop business. Despite a long leadership of the London scene, he's yet to demonstrate significant musical talent. *(LFI Ltd.)*

If the 'pretty boy' look is likely to pass, with it will go Wham. Sorry, lads. *(LFI Ltd.)*

Marilyn has to be one of the daftest acts we've ever seen in the British pop business. Without the vocal talent of George, Marilyn is just left with the drag! Despite huge hype, any obvious talent refuses to surface. *(LFI Ltd.)*

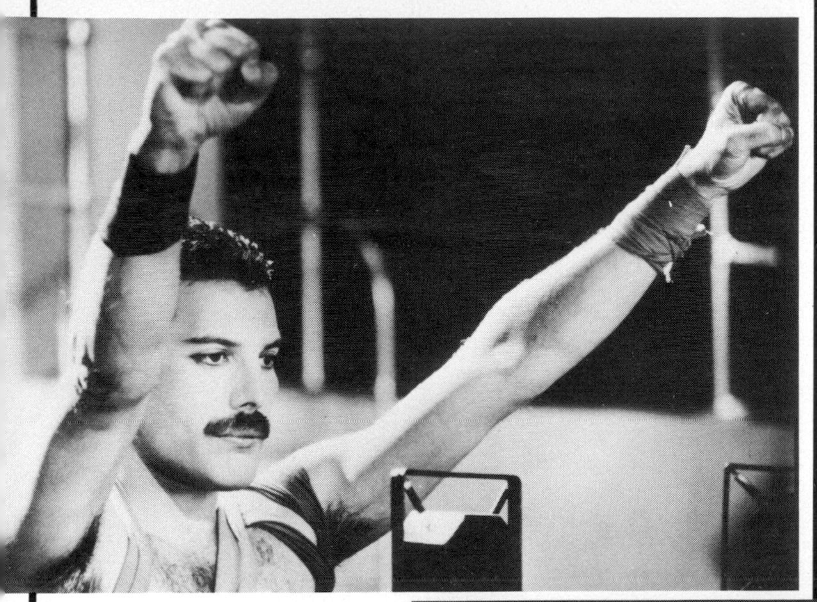

If you hate pop videos you can blame it all on Freddie and the Queen boys. They started the whole thing with their *Bohemian Rhapsody* tape in 1976 and, astonishingly, they are still managing to sell records ten years later — which is no bad thing as they're rather nice people! *(Simon Fowler/Queen Productions)*

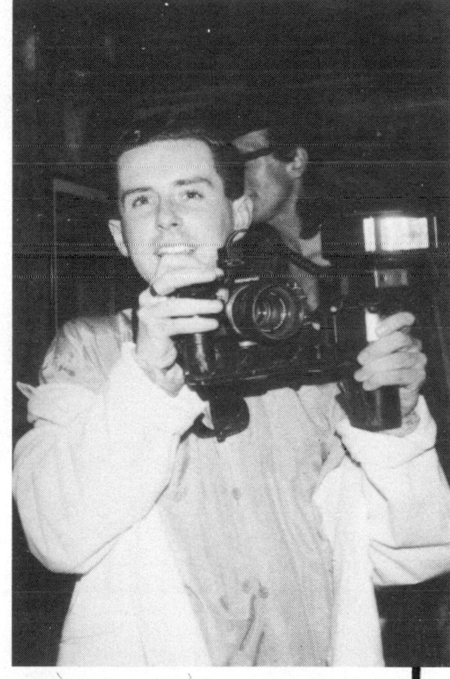

Here's Holly J. of FGTH, the band which most represents the new trend towards image consciousness. By superb marketing skill and production talent, Trevor Horne managed to create a massive industry from one good song — then the band had to learn how to play live!. *(LFI Ltd.)*

The Smiths avoid the extremes which can later rebound and, for this reason, might be able to hang on to success for more than just a year or so.
(Paul Cox/Rough Trade)

Tears for Fears are a British band who had to go to the USA to make it — or rather their videos had to go to the USA. With the help of MTV, the all-pop video cable station, TFF, had a hit in the USA and then the mighty business machinery swung behind them in an effort to put their records into the UK chart. It didn't fail!

two years. Certain things become a way of life. When you have to go to the airport the office always sends a limo: not a taxi, but a black Princess or Daimler limousine. Every time you have to go to the office the limo arrives. Every time you go for any appointment — an interview, the hairdresser, a photographer — the limo is there. All restaurant bills are taken care of by your road manager (or tour manager) and when there is heavy money flowing who wouldn't order champagne and invite loads of friends to join in? It's all natural.

So too is it natural for your manager to gather every single receipt, every single booking order for almost everything you spend and, often, for things you haven't bought. Unless you've hammered out who pays what in expenses in your management contract, you will be paying for everything out of *your* share.

After a two year period of travelling the world, stepping from limo, to plane, to limo, to hotel room, to stage and to bed it will be *impossible* for you to have a clear picture of what you have spent.

Who's to say whether you had 200 or 300 limo rides (at £120 a time!) in Britain last year? You can rely on the fact that the manager will have doubled up these expenses. Who's to say how much six suites at the Disneyland Hotel, Anaheim, California, really cost? You have the bills to look at but what else was charged to them? Do you have the accountant's eye for comparing detailed costs against an aggregate spent by the party in similar circumstances?

True financial reckoning between manager and artist will often not occur until the artist forces it, and then it will become a major showdown.

THE TWO-YEAR PERIOD

If a crooked manager is able to rip off an internationally successful act for two years, he will have recovered his investment and made a more than handsome profit. (Had he managed you fairly he would have made a reasonable profit). If you have managed to withstand the ego explosion, you will have been holding much of the cash you have been drawing and will be doing your best to mitigate the damage. At the end of two years, providing you have maintained your chart success (and the manager should have ensured this for his Golden Goose), you are in a position to bite the hand that has supposedly fed you, and turn the tables in quite a drastic way. This is the best way to plan a career as a successful pop performer if you suspect your management company of cheating you.

It is worth pointing out a few ways in which you can lessen the damage you will suffer in the first couple of years. If you do suspect your manager, you must be careful during this period not to show your hand too much, but, if you can manage it through the thrill of success, you ought to keep a diary of daily events. This doesn't have to be a commentary on what is happening, but it should list all travel and accommodation details:

8.30 Limo to airport
10. Plane to Frankfurt
Noon. Limo to Canadian Pacific hotel.
3pm Limo to studio
9pm Limo to hotel
Meals and drinks: approximately £400.
Overnight: Four suites for eleven people.
Etc

It is clearly difficult to keep track of expenses and the above outline is only the sort of expenditure which might be incurred when the band does a TV show in Germany: touring will be much more complex.

If you can manage to keep a log of this sort (and not lose it in a hotel bedroom during a party) you'll be doing a lot to lessen the final damage. When the question about dividing up residual earnings does arrive, mention the fact that you've kept a log of all movements before the actual accounts are produced. It could save you £50,000 before the arguments begin.

Another method of slowing down the take without upsetting things too much is to appoint your own accountant as soon as you suspect you are going to be ripped off (ideally from Day 1) and let it be known that you have done so. It isn't wise to insist that your accountant has access to all financial records concerning your career which are held by the management company unless your career is very secure. The risk is that for an artist with only one or two Top Ten hits, the manager has the option to withdraw support and effectively leave the artist in a contractual wilderness. This rarely happens in practice, but care must be exercised not to show your hand before your career is strong enough to support you.

One problem which makes for particular difficulty for bands managed by crooked managers is the reduction in the success cycle in the UK pop business. Bands are gaining massive popularity and losing it again over shorter and shorter time spans: currently around two years. This means that the long-term careers which have been enjoyed by such acts as the Rolling Stones, Status Quo or Queen, may not be available to the majority of bands making it today. For this reason it is impossible to collect as much money as possible from the first few hits since it is much less certain that careers can be sustained over many years.

This consideration indicates that an artist who is not happy with his or her financial position should take personal legal advice as soon as possible.

LENGTH OF CONTRACT

If you do decide to run the risk and sign with a manager, you can limit the damage that may be done by keeping the duration of the contract fairly short.

Until very recently managers refused to sign bands for less than five years, but as things have got tougher in the record business managers are now prepared to consider five year contracts which, like recording contracts, revolve around a specific number of album releases — four being the norm.

Try to get a two year agreement if you can, but if you don't have a record deal when you are negotiating your management contract you may have to accept three years or four albums as a compromise.

INDIVIDUAL SIGNING

Even though you might be just one part of a band that's being signed, you will have to sign all recording and management contracts as though you are a solo performer. This is understandable; without it a band could break up and leave the manager without a 'property'.

Be prepared virtually to sign away the rights to your life for the period of the contract; nearly all management agreements insist that managers have the power to make many career decisions on your behalf — often without reference or consultation.

HIT TIP

Don't give any manager your power of attorney!

A power of attorney allows a manager to sign contracts on your behalf, even if you don't know about them, and you can legally be forced to meet the terms of any such contract.

If any manager asks you to grant him power of attorney, refuse immediately and look for another manager.

As you will not be giving your manager power of attorney, all contracts agreed on your behalf by him will still have to be signed by you before they are valid. This gives you final control over your career, but it is often too late to stop harmful deals being agreed. However, if you employ a manager to manage your career you must obviously give him power to do so, so it is worth taking note of the amount of power you hand over when you sign a management contract.

While you are unsuccessful you will feel as though you are working for your manager. When you have achieved and sustained success you will begin to see your manager as an employee, working for you. This latter attitude is the correct one and you should try to develop it as early in your career as possible.

HOW MANY POINTS?

The average management contract grants a manager fifteen points (fifteen per cent) out of your gross earnings for the period, or number of records, stipulated in the contract. This is from your worldwide income, from all aspects: recording, touring, TV appearances, merchandizing, songwriting, book publishing, etc. Most management contracts stipulate that the manager will collect all monies for you, deduct his commission, and then pass the residue on to you. If you feel in a sufficiently strong position, you should try to have all monies paid to your accountant who will then pay the manager his percentage. This is difficult to arrange, however. Some managers might demand twenty points of your earnings, but you should resist until the problem of agents' fees has been agreed.

Agents normally charge a ten per cent booking fee for arranging concerts and obtaining gigs, but if two agents are involved this rises to fifteen per cent (the two agents splitting the commission between them). US agents charge fifteen per cent and if two agents are involved this rises to twenty per cent.

You don't have to be a genius to realize that on a US tour you could easily end up paying out 40 per cent of your take *before* you've started to pay expenses for the road crew, the sound equipment, the lighting, the travelling, the hotels, etc.

Managers usually act as agents these days — there are very few 'pure' booking agents left — and you must strive to get an agreement which limits your fees to a total of twenty points when only one agent (your manager) is involved and to 25 per cent when two agents are involved (including the US). This is quite important if you intend to make money out of live appearances.

'LOSS MAKING' TOURS

You will have frequently heard that bands on major tours lose money and that the only reason they tour is to promote their record sales. This is not true.

Most tours make money for the band and the promoters, but touring is the one area of the music business where cash is involved and it suits most successful bands to defray as many expenses against a tour budget as possible while pocketing the maximum amount of cash.

It is illegal for bands and managers to take cash sums and not declare them on their income tax returns, but the practice is endemic.

On tour, merchandizing can now gross almost as much as ticket receipts. Several thousand pounds can be taken each night of a tour from sales of posters, T-shirts, stickers, badges, belts, balloons, scarves, key rings, flags, ties, calendars, books and records and, not surprisingly, most of this cash finds its way into the manager's care. (Often a trusted tour manager will be deputized to look after franchising on a tour). Some gate money will be taken in cash (usually the 'on-the-night' sales) and much of this 'black' money ends up in private safes or in overseas bank accounts.

You should be aware of this for two reasons: first because it is an illegal practice and you might be unwittingly involved in such activity and, second, because you need to understand the nature of the business if you are to regulate your manager's take.

All of the tour expenses (and some expenses which may not be directly related to the tour) will be laid against the official gate receipts. The aim for most accountants is to produce a balance sheet from the tour which makes a sizeable loss. Such a loss can be placed against the income from recording and songwriting and can save tax in these areas.

There are other, much more devious, ways of extracting cash from live gigs, but providing the principle is understood, you should be armed to deal with those who, with a deadpan expression, assure you that live performances are poor business.

You can look at this another way: *if* major tours lost money, and *if* the main reason for touring is to sell records, you could legitimately expect the record company to meet a major share of tour expenses as they take the major profit from record sales. In rare instances this happens, but for the average tour, the accepted rule is to complain about the losses while stashing the profit in a safe place.

WHAT SHOULD A MANAGER DO FOR YOU?

If you are unknown when you sign a management agreement, a manager should turn you into a star. This involves seeking and negotiating a recording contract, helping to find the right producer, hiring record pluggers and promoters, motivating the record company and the sales reps, buying advertising, organizing fly posting, organizing the right sort of gigs, hiring a publicist and doing all that is necessary to get a record into the charts. Your manager becomes the driving force behind your success: he is the person who never takes the pressure off the record company, the pluggers, the publicists and anyone else who can help you.

Even though a successful manager will have much of the necessary machinery in place, he or she still needs to be a dynamo, a powerhouse who is a larger-than-life character. This type of person is extremely rare and if you find one of whom you feel confident, you will be very fortunate.

It is possible to sign to a manager and then discover he does nothing for you. This is unlikely if you have secured a good recording deal, but it might be useful to put performance guarantees into a contract to limit the time you are stuck with a non-performing manager. A lawyer will advise you about such clauses.

TROUBLE WITH YOUR MANAGER

According to music business statistics, you are almost certain to split from your first manager within five years and the split is likely to be acrimonious.

You can lessen the problems by being aware of this likelihood at the start and by carefully drawing up your management contract, but when people decide that they don't want to work together any more, there is nothing any contract can do to heal the rift. The spirit is much more powerful than words on a piece of paper.

Most problems between managers and artists are financial, with the artist nearly always the wounded party. The music press has been singularly short of headlines proclaiming 'Band cheated me, claims Manager'.

If you are very unlucky you might fall foul of a few villains in the business who do try strong-arm tactics. There were several such characters operating in the 1960s and 1970s, but most of them have been driven out by their own lack of professionalism.

If you are threatened with violence go immediately to the police. However bad the threats are, they are designed to be threats and any villain who issues 'warnings' clearly doesn't really want to hurt you (you may be too valuable in one piece). If a crook had wanted you hurt that would simply have happened.

There is absolutely no way that such a situation can be sorted out privately and if you do give in to threats you can be sure that life won't be worth living in the future. Nowadays threats are a very remote possibility, but if you are unlucky enough to suffer in this way, go immediately to the law, no matter what your prior relations with the police have been.

THE RIGHT BALANCE

Relations between managers and their artists seem better now than they have been for many years. This may be because the business is getting tougher and lawyers are beginning to eat into the managers' preserve.

There are several management companies in London who combine skilled career guidance with fair play and fair percentages and who, as a direct result, are inundated with requests for management from those who have already made it, let alone those who hope to be successful. Ask other musicians you meet on the road about their management experiences and when you keep hearing good reports about a particular name, make sure you get all the details.

You should do your best to interest those managers who are in the greatest demand. Persist in your attempts to get someone from their office to see your band, and keep sending them demos, because if you are lucky enough to get the right manager, all the doors, so long obstinately locked against you, will seem to open as though by magic.

6

THE PRODUCER AND THE SONG

With the right manager or lawyer and with the all-important record deal signed, you are two-thirds of the way towards making a hit. The two ingredients missing are a producer who has found out how to make hits and a song that is so strong that it would almost work without the 'priority' treatment. This is the ideal situation.

Many songs are now hits that would not make the charts were it not for the manipulation carried out by record companies, managers and pluggers, but finding a song that is a 'natural' hit will make the operation much easier.

THE PRODUCER

Twenty years ago there were no record producers, only 'A&R' (Artists and Repertoire) men. The mid-sixties spawned a whole host of independent record 'producers' who proved their hit-making ability so successfully that they were able to leave the security and shelter of the large record companies and sell their talents on a free-lance basis. These producers frequently set up their own production companies and signed acts to make records for their companies — rather than for the major record labels — and then leased the product they recorded to one of the major companies for a set period of years.

This seemed like a good idea in the years between 1966 and 1972 when there wasn't much of a market for 'Golden Oldies' and many of the major labels signed deals which allowed tracks to revert to the producers' companies after ten or fifteen years. At that time the thinking in the large companies was that pop music was a 'throw-away' item which would have little value ten years after it was a hit.

The enduring nature of Beatles' tunes, of tracks like *Whiter Shade of Pale* or *Hey Joe*, or of the Elvis recordings, have now proved that pop songs and recordings sometimes have a much longer life and, as a result, the mood of the industry changed.

By the mid-seventies there were fewer independents and more 'house producers' and the UK business shrugged off its old image of rich and flabby independent producers in favour of kids with 'street credibility' who were in tune with the new music rather than the sixties.

Today the pendulum has swung back in favoar of the producer who works independently.

However, the change is so profound this time, that there may never be a switch back to employed record producers. The contracting record market, and the degree of control now exercised over the charts by the few major record distributors, has combined to ensure that those producers with strong track records get an even larger share of a diminishing cake.

To put it crudely, there is no room for beginners; the hopes and aspirations of the New Wave generation for greater egalitarianism and redistribution of creative power in pop music have been dashed. The business is now, more than ever, in the control of the establishment and there are now fewer producers making more hits.

It is vital that you are produced by someone who has already produced hits. There is always the chance that you may find a new producer of such stunningly original ideas that he manages to force your record to the attention of the broadcast media by sheer brilliance, but the problem is that a major record company and/or management company are not likely to invest the hundreds of thousands of pounds needed to ensure chart success if the product itself is going to be created by someone who has yet to prove he can make successful products.

For this reason, the successful producers such as Martin Rushent, Trevor Horn, Steve Levine, Steve Lillywhite, Chris Neil, Nick Tauber and Pip Williams, are always in demand and are able to state their own terms.

If you've managed to get a recording deal without having a producer, the next stage will be for you, your manager (if you have one) and your record company executive to discuss which type of producer is right for your band or act.

You may admire a particular producer's work and if everyone agrees that his sound is right for you, an approach will be made to see if he's interested in the band.

Most producers are very cautious before agreeing to produce new acts and if they like the sound of your demo they will come and see you play live or meet you in a studio. It's rather like having to audition all over again.

HIT TIP

If you've done your homework and prepared a list of which record companies and labels have been most successful, it is also worth doing your own chart of the producers. *Music Week* publishes the producers' names against chart records each week and if you take the magazine regularly, you will soon see which producers are most successful and who produces the sort of record you admire.

Based on *Music Week*'s own figures, here is the 'Top Ten' of producers (complied from chart performance for the first part of 1984).

1. Trevor Horn
2. Peter Collins
3. James Anthony Carmichael/Lionel Richie
4. Alex Sadkin/Tom Bailey
5. Reinhold Heil/Manne Praeker
6. Kool & The Gang
7. Rupert Hine
8. Queen/Mack
9. Rick Chertoff
10. Phil Ramone

Music Week's album chart produces a different profile of producers which amply illustrates how different the album market has become from the singles market:

1 Alex Sadkin/Tom Bailey
2 Quincy Jones
3 Phil Ramone
4 James Anthony Carmichael/Lionel Richie
5 Steve Lillywhite
6 David A. Stewart
7 Laurie Latham
8 Rupert Hine
9 Jimmy Lovine
10 Steve Levine

(Also check Bert Muirhead's *The Record Producers File*, Blandford Press, 1984).

If a producer thinks he can do something with you in the studio he'll open up negotiations. If not, he'll pass up the chance of the money and move on to something else. Hit producers can't afford to produce records which might flop, or at least do less well than 'priority' treatment should indicate.

PAYING THE PRODUCER

Most producers ask for around two and a half to three per cent of the record they produce. A few ask for a percentage of the band's entire earnings for the year and, demonstrating how powerful the producer has become, all hit-making producers ask for an advance on their royalties.

This is a relatively new development; remember that the producer's advance and royalties will have to come from your money. Good producers are regularly getting £5,000 for producing a single and many are getting £10,000 and even £20,000. In a few cases higher figures are paid. Albums aren't normally produced until a single has reached a good position in the chart (in 1972 the singles market was scorned by the 'serious' bands who made a long (and usually boring) album immediately after signing a recording deal), but a producer's album advance may very well be £30,000.

So, out of their (typical) nine points, the band has to give away 2.5 to a producer leaving them with 6.5 to split between the band members. If they've received a £100,000 advance, £20,000 of it may very well go to a producer. It is worth it, however. The right producer will mould you in ways you may not think possible. To some extent your early recordings may become reflections of his talent rather than yours, but that is the current mood of the business.

The most important aspect of choosing a producer is to work with someone you like and you respect musically. Nearly all producers are either musicians and/or ex-studio engineers so you'll be working with someone who understands your feelings very well.

Producers are often employed on one record at a time, but if you get on well with a particular producer who makes hit records for you, then a long-term working relationship is likely to develop which will benefit all concerned.

PRODUCING YOURSELVES

Occasionally a new band strikes a record deal which lets them produce their own masters. This happened quite a lot in the early 1970s, but it is now quite rare.

If you have no studio experience it is very unwise to take this option, even if it is offered. You may like the idea of having creative freedom and total control over your own recordings, but you won't have the experience to make the most of your talent. You won't be in a position to know the options available to you in a studio and you can't rely on a studio engineer, however good, to think up creative alternatives for you.

Consider a co-production deal if you can negotiate it. This will save you a couple of percentage points and will give you considerable control, but you will have to find an experienced producer and you will have to persuade him to work with you. As hit producers already have more work than they can handle this may not be easy.

If your band is made up of experienced musicians with considerable studio time behind them, it is feasible for you to produce yourselves. The trick in this situation is to find yourself a really top-class engineer with whom you feel a rapport. His role will be to provide the technical expertise while you concentrate on the music.

THE SONG

The song for your first A-side is all-important. Despite the fact that the charts are largely manipulated, your success will come more easily if you've recorded a strong composition. It's fair to say that if your first A-side turns out to be weak you may very well not get priority treatment at all, although if you've been lucky enough to secure a large advance, it is likely that you'll be sent back into the studio to spend more of it on trying again.

If you managed to secure your recording deal on the strength of your songwriting (always the best way to do it), you and your producer may have no trouble picking the song which will be your first A-side: in fact, you may have too many to choose from. This is a happy state to be in.

If, however, you've been signed on the strength of your stage act, or a voice, or on the strength of a following, you may have to start looking elsewhere for possible songs to record.

There are many good reasons to try and use your own songs, however, and not the least of these is money. The income from publishing is usually outside the reach of managers (except the more unscrupulous ones) which has ensured that many new artists actually see something of the money they are generating. Management contracts usually stipulate that a percentage of your songwriting income is paid to the manager, but unless he controls the publishing company, the payouts will come directly to you, rather than from his office.

PUBLISHING DEALS

Song publishing is another aspect of the music business which has re-shaped itself drastically over the last few years under pressure from a contracting market.

Up until the late 1950s, song publishing was a major and vigorous part of the UK music business and for many years (before the widespread popularity of record players) it dominated the business. In the 1960s it grew into a flabby and apathetic industry with publishing houses taking 50 per cent of songwriters' income in return for doing *nothing*.

The traditional split of income between songwriter and song publisher was long established as 50/50, but this reflected the days when publishers actually printed and distributed sheet music out of their share of the income. As the sales of sheet music dwindled to almost nothing in the sixties, publishers took longer and longer lunches and moved into larger and larger offices.

Once a songwriter was established, publishers reluctantly agreed to re-shape publishing deals to set up a new publishing company in which the songwriter had a 50 per cent interest. In this way the songwriter received 75 per cent of his income; for a few years this seemed reasonable enough. Paul Simon was the first writer to secure this deal for himself in 1964 when he set up Pattern Music under the auspices of Lorna Music in London.

Today song publishers have been found out. Songwriters with some hits to their credit have discovered that the only work a publisher does is to sign a contract and collect money from the Performing Rights Society and other bodies. Most deals now start at 75 per cent for the songwriters (often through a new publishing company being established) and the most successful writers are able to screw the parasitic publishers down to take a mere ten per cent as a 'collection fee'.

Publishers, in turn, have now had to start working again. Over the last twenty years or so they forgot how to hawk songs around, but they're learning again and learning fast.

One of the most interesting developments is that bands who write their own material and who secure major recording deals are also getting large advances from publishers anxious to build their song catalogues; sums as high as £30,000, £50,000 and even £100,000 are not uncommon in the UK today.

This is another major source of income for musicians able to write well. If you write your own material, send it to music publishers as well as record companies. A list of publishers and their addresses appears in Appendix 2 at the back of this book.

FINDING A HIT SONG

Your producer will normally take on the task of finding a song for you to record. Even if you write your own songs it is he, in collaboration with your executive at the record company and, perhaps, your manager, who will pick the number which will eventually become your first A-side. Record label executives like to get involved, but the final choice is nearly always left to the producer.

If you don't write songs, or if none of your songs are considered suitable, the producer will have to set about finding hit songs for you and he will usually turn to writers who have already written hits for him. This is another reason for making sure the producer you work with has a track record: as well as being able to bestow the all-important 'aura' of hit making around you, he also has access to people who have proved they can write hits and those people know he can turn their songs into hits. For this reason he has access to songs lesser producers might not have.

In the days of A&R men, the recording manager used to stalk Tin Pan Alley (London's Denmark Street) visiting publishers to hear the latest offerings from each publishing house's songwriters. Today publishers have gone on the offensive and successful producers are now constantly being offered songs for consideration.

It can be a very worthwhile experience to find a successful writer who is inspired to write something specifically for your act. This type of arrangement was common in the 1960s when writers of the standard of Graham Gouldman, Tony Macauly and Barry Mason, Carole King and Dozier/Holland/Dozier were creating songs tailored specifically to fit individual types of recording artist. This type of approach has come back into style and if you're lucky enough to find a hit writer you can work with, don't hesitate to do so.

EGO PROBLEMS

If you write songs in the band, you will naturally be upset if the producer and your manager try to persuade you to record someone else's song as your A-side. Despite the above comments about advisability of recording your own material if at all possible, try to keep your ego out of it, and try not to be too hurt. Providing your production and management team has experience of making hits you can be sure they will only be asking you to record another number for the best reasons. If they were confident of making your own number into a hit they would do so in a flash: their earnings would be considerably higher and your reputation, as both performer *and* songwriter, would be greater.

The only exception to this rule is when a producer or manager wants you to record *his* song.

It has long been a dodge in the music business for managers and producers to hoist their songs on luckless bands signed to them for recording. The only time you should consider recording a song written by your manager or producer is when he has written previous hits (and hits within the last five years, not in 1968!). In this instance count yourself lucky to have a hit songwriter working with you.

In all other situations reject all approaches; go out and find your own song if necessary.

If you discover that your producer wants you to record someone else's song rather than yours, bide your time in the knowledge that the process will help you to become a better songwriter.

RE-ARRANGEMENTS

Each year there are now half a dozen re-makes of old hits which manage to enter the charts. Recently hits from the 1960s seemed to be the most popular; whatever era is the vogue, there is certainly a wealth of songs to choose from. The problem is, that you've got to improve on the original version in some way. Many of today's DJs and radio producers were playing the songs the first time around and if your version adds nothing to the song, then you'll have harmed your reputation for future releases.

For this reason, it is wise to consider covering an old hit only when it gains something from modernization. Some songs are so redolent of the 1960s that they can never sound like anything else: imagine trying to re-record Scott McKenzie's *San Francisco (Be Sure to Wear Flowers in Your Hair)*! Other songs are more transportable, however, and can benefit from being placed in a newer, more modern setting.

TEST MARKETING

If you are considering reworking an old song with a new arrangement, you really ought to test the market reaction to it. Most new products are tested in some way; every advertising agency which is asked to handle the launch of a new product, tests it by giving free samples to the type of person at whom the product is aimed and gathering their reactions. It makes excellent sense to do the same thing with a song.

If you're a working band you're provided with an ideal opportunity each night. If you have a reasonable audience you should be able to tell from their reaction what they think of any particular song in the set. Beware that live gigs tend to favour up-tempo action songs much more than air play would and you should apply the same sort of 'weighting' to your consideration of audience reaction as Gallup does when it compiles the chart returns.

Don't hesitate to ask your audience what they think of individual numbers. Not only on stage, but off stage too. Although you may have other things on your mind when you pick up a girl after a gig, you wouldn't be wasting your time if you found out what she (and her sisters around the country) feel about the numbers they've heard.

Some bands choose to sell high-quality demos of their recordings at their live gigs. This is a little 'small time' in approach and, if you've been lucky enough to get the right management and record deal, you should have left this behind you. Despite this, if you have had any experience of selling your own twelve inch singles or albums at gigs, you should have got some feel for which numbers prove most popular with the audiences. Don't ignore this feedback and do make a point of passing the information on to your producer. Although you're going to be a 'priority' act and are almost certain of getting your record into the charts, the stronger the song, the stronger and more lasting its success. It is always easier to hype a good product than a bad one. There used to be a rather smug and self-satisfied saying in the music business: 'You can only hype a good song.' That's not true any more, but the choice of song is still crucial to long-term success.

FINDING YOUR OWN SONGS

If you're in a deal which gives you lots of creative freedom, you may be able to cast your net far and wide to find good songs and get personally involved with their selection. A small ad in the back of *Melody Maker* will net you hundreds – mostly rubbish – but you never know. You might have far more joy getting hold of American tracks and listening to them. There are many specialist charts in America and if you get *Billboard*, the American music business magazine, you can watch the progress of certain songs and check them out to see if they might suit you. American songs aren't often 'covered' these days (once it was endemic), but it still happens from time to time and British artists still break into the charts with American songs, beating the original recording artists to UK chart success.

DEVELOPING YOUR SONGWRITING TALENT

If you are lucky enough to write songs which your producer thinks good enough for an A-side, you'll be astonished at what happens to your songwriting after the first record is released. I've interviewed many hit songwriters over the years and they all report the same phenomenon: making hits creates other hits.

While you're still unknown and struggling, you are writing songs in a vacuum, hoping that they will be hits, but aware in your subconscious mind that it is unlikely that your dreams are unlikely to become a reality. Once one of your songs starts climbing the charts, the psychological effect on your writing is tremendous and it can release all the bottled-up talent and inspiration within you.

From reading this book you'll be aware that your song will almost certainly have been made popular artificially at the beginning, but you should also know that once your song is in the Top Ten the real sales returns which follow indicate how that section of the public which has not been hyped feel about your song. If you have a sustained run with your first hit, it will be likely to push a thousand ideas for new songs into your mind, even while you are on the merry-go-round of interviews, photographs and TV appearances. This was never better demonstrated than by Lennon and McCartney during the period 1963-67. During this period they lived a life which most creative artists would consider sheer hell. They never had a moment to themselves and they were always travelling. In addition they were stars of a magnitude that is unimaginable today (youth had little other than music to interest them at that period) but the number and quality of songs they turned out in that four year period is staggering. Hit begets hit, if there's some talent there to start with.

7

MAKING THE MASTER

Recording a master track intended for an A-side is a completely different experience to recording a demo. Depending on the type of producer you have, you are likely either to be routined until you have grown to hate the song, or you will have far less rehearsal for it than you had when you were recording demos.

Studio time ceases to be a problem when you go into the studio to record a track which will become 'priority' for a record label; the only thing that matters is that the final sound is right.

CHOOSING THE STUDIO

You may be allowed quite a lot of say in choosing which studio to work in; alternatively, your producer may know one particular studio which is right for the sort of sound he wants to get on your record.

There are now many types of master studio available – from those situated in remote country houses to those in the back streets of central London. You'll get a more relaxed atmosphere if you choose to work in the country, but in the last few years there has been a swing back to city studios after a long period in which almost every band took itself off to a country retreat for a week or so.

Wherever you record, you can be sure that you will be recording in one of the major studios and almost every possible facility, from Fairlight synthesizer to digital mixdown will be available.

It is natural that artists new to recording should feel both nervous and excited about going into a first league studio to record a master. The novelty soon wears off, however, and studio recording is revealed for the very hard work it is.

HIT TIP

Studio time is very expensive in the big league — £100 an hour or more is not unusual — and as you'll probably buy four or five days for your first single, the bill could easily be £3,000 or £4,000. Many singles cost much more.

Remember that it is your money which is paying for the studio time in most instances. You may not be asked to pay the bill on the spot, but recording costs will either have to come out of the advance you've already received or out of royalties you will be paid in the future.

If you've received any message so far from this book, it must be that the musician and his money are soon parted, so it makes excellent sense to start as you mean to go on by trying to avoid gross extravagancy in the hiring of a studio.

It is understandable that you will want nothing but the best for the recording of your first master, but it is precisely this sort of feeling which makes musicians vulnerable to being fleeced.

The amount of work available for recording studios fluctuates and it is worthwhile shopping around for prices, if your producer doesn't mind. Ask one of your assistants to ring half a dozen of the top studios and get a quote for the amount of time you expect to spend and don't be above ringing them back and asking if they can improve on the quote. It could save you £1,000 by making one phone call.

Concentration is the most important quality required of those who work in recording studios and if you're not directly concerned with the production of the record, it can be an enormous aid to freshness to get out of the studio when you're not actually needed for recording.

If you can, get out of the entire studio complex; go for a walk —

sitting around the studio cafe or reception isn't the same.

It is natural that on your first master recording you will want to hang around and see everything, but it is very easy to get stale in a studio and a half hour break can work wonders for the feel of a track.

RECORDING WHEN THE 'MAGIC' IS IN THE AIR

Some old hands at sound engineering insist that they could always tell when a hit song was being recorded: they say there was a magic in the air, a sort of electricity which marked the occasion out as being different from the normal run-of-the-mill sessions.

In the light of the 'controlled' chart this theory doesn't really hold up today, but it is true that when things start to go exceptionally well on a session the lift tends to make everyone expectant, and perform just that little bit better.

Unfortunately, there's no automatic way of ensuring that you record when the electricity is in the air. You may recall the great love scenes played on film: Bogart and Bacall, Taylor and Burton, etc. The electricity which flowed between these couples — who were in love off screen as well as on — is almost visible on the celluloid. Recordings made on famous sessions have an equally tangible but indefinable air to them. You can't explain what it is, but there's a magic in the air.

The fact that you've secured a good recording deal and that you're going in to record your first master (which, you are assured, is very likely to go into the charts) should be enough to start you off with the right feel. Your producer should be able to monitor how the session is going, but you should know not to continue if you start to feel lousy, or if you know that there has been an unacceptable compromise made somewhere along the way during the recording.

All recording is compromise: there's always a time when you feel like saying, 'We won't bother to do that over, no one will notice in the final mix.' Very often small mistakes in the background instrumentals are not significant in the final mix, but sometimes a combination of little errors builds up to put a tarnish on the whole product. Watch for these, even though it is really your producer's job and, if necessary, be quite insistent about playing the part again if you haven't quite got it right. Don't be afraid to say 'No, I want to do it again.' You have this as an absolute right in the recording studio.

USING OTHER MUSICIANS

It is a time-honoured device in the recording industry to use session musicians to replace poor, or time-consuming, band members. The record is then put out under the band's name, hoodwinking the public into believing the band created the track on its own.

HIT TIP

Session men are a regenerated species. For many years they were regarded as the hacks of the music business, lugubriously strolling from studio to studio to make cardboard music.

Today the old-style session man has been largely replaced by young, enthusiastic musicians who have a strong feel for the music they play. Some of these new session players may not be able to read music, but if they're getting a living from recordings, they can obviously produce exciting music in the studio. Unless you are completely purist about your performance, don't hesitate to use them if your band needs augmenting in the studio.

If your producer wants to do this don't complain, so long as the entire band is not replaced. Remember how many now famous musicians never played on their first records. It is often just a matter of expediency for the producer to use musicians he knows will give him an exact sound. It doesn't necessarily mean he doesn't think you're good enough to play the part, it's just that you won't have worked with him long enough to be able to know precisely how to achieve the effect required.

DRUGS IN THE STUDIO

If there's one place a band may feel like using recreational drugs — and alcohol is probably top of the list — it's in the recording studio. Nervousness is natural, especially when you're recording your first master tracks, but any drug will impair your abilities during the basic stages of recording. Remember the warning mentioned in Chapter 3: a half pint of lager removes a human's ability to hear above 16K — you won't be able to hear the true balance of the cymbals in a drum kit mix — and other drugs destroy perception in various degrees.

The only case that can be made out for 'relaxants' in the studio is for the final vocals. Extreme nervousness can get in the way of a relaxed performance or it can stop it reaching its full potential in some way. Caution is needed here, however, as the same stimulant or relaxant which can improve your performance will also take away your ability to judge it objectively.

If you usually function in a high state the foregoing won't apply as 'high' has become your 'normal' state. For all others, the general rule is to avoid stimulants in the studio. The recording session itself is usually able to provide all of the adrenalin required and if it doesn't you can take it as a sure sign that the end product won't be much good.

SAYING 'NO'

Having made the point that the producer is all-important in the manufacture of a hit record, it is also fair to say that the recording studio is the one place where the artist really matters. It is *your* music and/or song which is the raw material from which everything grows.

If you've had a chance to work out the numbers with your producer before going into the studio, you shouldn't suffer any nasty surprises, but if you find that either he or the engineer does want to do something that you disagree with profoundly, you shouldn't hesitate to say so. In the recording studio your opinion matters.

If a debate over a musical or a production point reaches stalemate, the only reasonable approach is to take a democratic decision with all involved parties voting. If the producer won't accept this you may be forced to accede, unless you feel the point is fundamental to the entire recording.

It is very rare that this situation occurs since it is part of a producer's job to ensure that it doesn't. However, bear in mind that the studio is one of the two places where the musician really matters (the other is on stage) and you shouldn't be frightened of saying 'no' if it is absolutely necessary.

WORKING WITH THE RIGHT ENGINEER

Choosing the right engineer for the master session is really your producer's job. Some of the most important aspects of the relationship between engineer and recording artists have been mentioned in Chapter 3 with regard to making a demo.

Despite this, the engineer has an all-important role in the making of a master and with the backing of a record company you are in a position to pick and choose which engineer you would like to use.

Unlike the practices of the small demo studios, the consoles in the large studios are operated mainly by independent engineers who move from studio to studio, mastering all the different technical problems they meet with an ease which is only born of long experience.

You can expect your producer to use an engineer with whom he has worked before — a sensible arrangement. You have to be able to get along with the engineer as well, so it is reasonable for you to ask to meet him before you go into the studio for the master session. Bear in mind that most of the dialogue during the session will be between the producer and engineer, but you will benefit from greater involvement if you have taken the trouble to get to know the engineer in advance.

THE RECORDING

Try to stay calm even if the actual recording turns out to be a nightmare. If you're working with a producer who is new to you you'll be taking orders about your music for the first time and it may not seem like a very pleasant experience.

There are two personal qualities which are of great importance in the recording studio: patience and concentration. If you're not involved in the actual production decisions, you'll need a lot of the former; if you are producing or co-producing you'll need the latter.

There's a lot of waiting involved in recording: waiting until the engineer has got his sounds right; waiting while other musicians struggle to play their part in precisely the right way; and a lot of waiting which doesn't seem to be for any good reason.

The concentration is needed when you are struggling to get one paricular part right. After listening to a solo twenty times it becomes very difficult to decide which is the best take. It is here that a producer should prove his worth. Concentration seems to be the one single common denominator that is discernible among hit producers. They never seem to tire of hearing the same part and they seem to retain an enthusiasm for the process of recording long after most normal mortals would have screamed and thrown a tantrum.

The part of the session in which the actual recording takes place is comparable to the building of foundations for a house. However marvellous the mix and vocals might be, if the back track recording is poor the whole record will feel wrong.

MIXING

Mixing is probably the most exciting part of a recording session as it is the first time that those involved begin to hear how the finished product will sound. Mixing can also be a long drawn out affair, even if you do your best to avoid tedious mixes which usually lack sparkle.

Computer-controlled mixing desks have taken a great deal of the sweat out of reduction, as it is called in the trade, and if your producer allows you to attend the mix you should find it a very enjoyable experience.

Don't be too hurt if your producer wants to mix it alone. It is much better to get a mix which is one person's image of a song than to get a 'committee' feel to the product. Everyone has their own ideas about mixing and resolving conflicts by compromise can undermine the strength of the track.

HIT TIP

Before you get down to making the final mix of your first tracks it is worth taking a rough mix away and testing it on friends, fans and relations.

This type of input can help you regain objectivity about the A-side track — you'll be thoroughly sick of it by the time the recording is finished — and it is vital you have this before mixing begins.

The concept of 'test marketing' was mentioned earlier in this chapter, and this type of market analysis is now becoming widespread.

During the seventies marketing companies used to test subjects with sensors to see how they reacted to certain records. By measuring the physical responses of the skin and muscles, experts claimed to be able to tell when the test subjects heard a record they particularly liked.

Not surprisingly, these methods are now out of favour, but sophisticated test methods are still being used. The current fashion is to play forthcoming releases to record buyers and then ask questions about the records. By including questions about which magazines the record buyers read and what radio and TV broadcasts they hear and watch, the marketing men try to build up an 'ideal' marketing strategy for each single. And so the hit making machine finally arrives at the point where all of the manipulative power and knowledge at its disposal has to be put into one area, promotion!

8

PROMOTION AND THE CHARTS

Promotion is probably the most important single word in the entire vocabulary of the record business.

In order to get a single into the charts it has to be heavily promoted – to the music press, the broadcast media, the record shop trade and to the general public. Making a hit demands 100 per cent effort in all of these avenues at once. Promotion can be split into the following categories:

1 The Music press.
2 The national press.
3 Local press.
4 National radio.
5 Local radio.
6 Pirate radio.
7 National TV.
8 Regional TV.
9 Clubs and discos (where appropriate).
10 The record company sales staff.
11 The record shops.
12 The general public.

MARKET CONSIDERATIONS

Advertising men now describe the pop music market as being 'closely targeted'. This means that there is a narrow, easily identifiable group of people who regularly buy pop records.

Over the last ten years the pattern of record buying has changed beyond recognition. In the mid-seventies the typical pop record buyer was anywhere between 15 and 45 and he or she would buy records occasionally. Those who bought records frequently bought one a week but more normally a record was a monthly purchase.

Today the majority of people who buy chart singles are between fourteen and nineteen and heavy record buyers purchase three or four records a week, each! One a week is average. Once again, pop has become a cult which is purely of youth. Few people in their twenties and thirties buy singles today, although there are occasionally records which are described as 'crossover' records which manage to attract buyers outside of this age group. Artists with this power include names like Stevie Wonder and Lionel Richie. The result of this changed pattern is that the main record buyers can be clearly identified; it is this factor which has made the charts so ripe for manipulation.

When records were bought across a twenty year age span it was much more costly for marketing people to reach a sizeable proportion of the buyers. Now that they are mostly slotted into one group with a five year age span, it has become much easier. This is the most important single factor which has produced Britain's vulnerable chart situation.

In order to reach this group of record buyers, the marketing directors of the record companies examine the media used by this group and look to see which forms of advertising achieve the maximum exposure to the teenage market.

If you are aiming at this market, every part of your image should have been shaped with this particular group of record buyers in mind. You should have a very clear mental picture of the type of person who will buy your record and most of your public activity should be directly aimed at captivating him or her.

Image is such an intangible element in an act's presentation that it is impossible to set down any rules for it. The moment such a rule is suggested someone can prove how effective it can be to break it. We must assume that the image you and/or your management have developed appeals to this teenage market and that you have read their response correctly.

THE MUSIC PRESS

The vast changes in the nature of Britain's pop music market are accurately reflected in the changes forced on the structure of the British pop music press.

Since the early 1960s the British music press has been the envy of the world's music business and it continues to be so. No other country — including the USA — has publications to equal those produced in Britain.

There are currently seven main music papers — six published weekly, one fortnightly — and their combined circulation tops one million copies. Most papers are read by several people besides the purchasers so it is easy to see that there are several million people in Britain who wish to read about pop music and fashion.

At the time of writing, *Smash Hits* is the most successful music paper in the UK, selling 478,000 copies every two weeks. *No. 1*, selling 211,000 weekly, can be considered equally successful and these two new papers are followed by the long-established favourites, *New Musical Express* and *Sounds*, with 123,000 and 93,000 weekly copies respectively.

For the years between 1963 and 1978, *Melody Maker* was considered Britain's premier music paper and in the late sixties its circulation figures exceeded half a million. It now sells around 66,000 copies a week; this dramatic turn-around indicates the profound shift in fashion which has occurred in the music business.

ADVERTISING

There are two ways of reaching the readers of the music papers. The first is to advertise, the second is to try to persuade the editor and reporters to run editorial copy on you.

Advertising is necessary for a new act with a priority single. Nobody in the music business believes that advertising actually sells records: a record is, after all, a sound medium and you can't show a picture to sell a sound. If a band has a particularly unusual image, newspaper ads can have an effect on selling that image, but ads sell the band name rather than individual records.

Despite this, advertising is a vital ingredient in any major campaign. A whole page advertisement in the more successful music papers costs several thousand pounds and your record company and/or management will want to take lots of page ads in the papers which most closely fit your image just to let the trade know that yours is a priority record. Spending a large sum on what on the face of it may seem fairly useless advertising is one of the main methods of telling the record trade that your record is going to be priority.

All record shop owners scan the music press and their ordering decisions are based on the effort they see reflected in those pages. In addition to the advertising campaign in the consumer music press, the record company will also launch a campaign in *Music Week*, the music business's trade paper, and this will make it clear to record shop owners that the label means business with your single. It is impossible to mount a serious promotional campaign without a significant advertising budget.

Buying the space for the ads isn't the only expense. The job of creating the ads to fit your image and to have the maximum effect has to be handled by professionals in an advertising agency; this work is also likely to cost thousands of pounds. At the end of the day, your first single is likely to be supported by a number of different ads which appear for three or four weeks immediately after release in the most successful music papers. Whether you end up paying for these ads and their preparation out of your advance — typically costing around £10,000 — depends on the terms of your recording contract. This is yet another indication that you should be very careful over the terms agreed (see Chapter 4).

GETTING EDITORIAL

Editorial coverage is believed to be four times as effective as normal newspaper advertising; persuading a paper to carry a double page feature about you can be reckoned to be worth many thousands of pounds.

The problem is how to make it happen.

Step one is for your record company or management to hire a publicist. There are many freelance publicists in London who specialize in making this connection. They've been working in the business for a long time and have got to know most of the journalists and editors working in the music press. Their job is to get you editorial coverage in the papers — newspapers and magazines as well as the music press — and they do this by being on personal terms with the journalists.

It is very useful if you have London gigs organized to coincide with the release of your record. This gives the publicist an excellent chance of getting a reporter down to see you. The publicist can't make the journalist like you, but his or her knowledge of the individual reporters' tastes should tell him or her which are likely to be most sympathetic to your type of music.

HIT TIP

Making people believe that 'something is happening' is the main aim of any promotion campaign. To some extent it is a job of mirrors, using reflections to make you, and your record, seem greater than it actually is.

If a journalist on *Sounds* thinks you are a hot property and the publicist offers him the chance to see you before someone from *NME* gets the chance, you are more likely to spring that little mental switch which makes the reporter believe he is witnessing the birth of something important. Before this starts to sound too cynical, it is fair to point out that on occasion he actually might be.

Publicists secure their relationship with music press reporters by bribery. No money changes hands, but journalists are 'looked after' exceedingly well. They are regularly taken on 'all-expenses paid' trips to exotic locations to see acts play live or in the recording studio and most publicists supply cocaine as and when necessary, again free of charge.

Hiring a publicist to work this magic on your behalf isn't cheap. It will cost (and, yes it will probably come out of your advance) between £500 and £1,000 a week, and you are likely to need the machine to work for you for six weeks or so.

The music press journalists will also be hyped to your name by the advertisements appearing in their papers. Because the publicist working on your behalf will be one of the most successful, the journalists will begin to get the message that something special is happening.

As well as working on the music press, the publicist also has the job of trying to get national newspaper coverage for you. This is much more difficult; Fleet Street journalists are less open to the sort of thinly-veiled bribery which works with writers in the music press. The only way a piece will appear in the *Daily Mirror* or *Daily Mail* about you or your band is if the story is good enough. For this you will need to have had a sex change operation, to have been banned in America's bible belt or to have had an affair with a Royal.

From time to time 'puffs' on bands do scrape into the nationals. Puffs are stories which are just promotional pieces and these 'fillers' are usually reserved for the blank news weeks of the 'silly season' in mid-summer. Don't bank on the likelihood of your publicist getting you any coverage in the nationals. This isn't of vital importance as your 'target group' don't read any of the national newspapers in discernible quantities. Most of the attention should go into reaching them through their own media — the music press, radio and pop TV.

The last job your publicist will have will be to ensure you get local and regional newspaper coverage. This will be easy in your home area and difficult elsewhere — until the record starts to show in the charts. Once again, it doesn't matter greatly as your target doesn't pay much attention to local papers.

Getting the first 'chart showing' is the all-important key to the door. This allows newspapers and radio DJs to describe the record as a 'hit' and provides the excuse for everyone to put their shoulder to the bandwagon. Getting that entry is the single most important element in any promotion campaign and all your promotion team — the ad agency, the publicist, the pluggers, the record company sales team — hang on that showing. This is why so much effort goes into getting your record into the right shops — as discussed in the later section, 'Marketing'.

RADIO

Airplay is all-important. A record is made to be heard and the best avenue for exploitation is to have it played regularly on the radio. There are three main types of radio outlet: national, local and pirate. It may well be that by the time you read this, pirate radio will have suffered from another major clamp-down by the government and only be of minor importance. To judge by Continental developments, however, the spread of inexpensive broadcasting technology is making it easier for the pirates and harder for governments, and pirate radio could maintain its important, if insidious, role in music promotion.

National air-play means only one thing: the BBC, and in particular Radio 1. There is a plan for a national independent radio channel, but it is not yet clear how high pop music, and in particular chart music, will be on its list of priorities. At the time of writing it seems unlikely that music would be the major part of its output.

Records played on Radio 1 programmes are chosen by BBC producers with some influence from the DJs themselves. The better known the DJ the more likely he or she is to have a strong say in what is played.

There seems to be no direct bribery or old-fashioned payola at work inside the BBC at present, but indirect influence continues unabated. The key figure in terms of your air-play will be your record plugger.

THE PLUGGER

Every major record company has a team of promotion men and women called record pluggers. Their job is to supply radio stations with records and do their best to persuade producers and DJs to play their records. It is a very tough job.

HIT TIP

Many pluggers have now organized themselves into large-scale companies with a full team to ensure national coverage. They can often boast an in-field team of between twelve and fifteen pluggers who work on local TV and radio, while the heavyweight boss plugger concentrates on London media.

In addition to 'plugging', promotion companies organize DJ mailing of records and ensure that the right clubs and discos are canvassed. Many firms also get involved in in-store appearances and promotion; from now on when you read 'plugger' you should understand that he usually has a heavyweight organization behind him.

At the lowest level, record pluggers are merely delivery boys, dropping records into radio offices and exchanging pleasantries. At the highest, they are formidable personalities who deal in cocaine and are privy to the private world inhabited by the rock superstars and magnates.

If your record is to be 'priority' you will almost certainly end up hiring an independent plugger to work on your behalf. Even though your record company will have its own team of full-time pluggers, the employment of a well-known and powerful independent plugger is yet another sign to DJs and producers that your act is 'something special'. They will have already seen the press ads and read the articles your publicist has procured for you in the music press; now they will realize that one of the best London pluggers has been hired to work on your record. It adds a great deal to the climate in which a record is first heard.

In precisely the same way that unsolicited demos are listened to in a negative way in record company offices, so new singles released without any support also receive 'uninterested' hearings in the producers' offices at radio stations and at the various play-list panels which are constituted from time to time. On the other hand, a buzz in the business that a particular band or artist is getting priority treatment from a major record company will normally ensure that the record is listened to much more carefully. This is an understandable human reaction. If a producer knows that the business is pumping money into an act, he will want to make sure that he is not missing anything important. Even if he doesn't like the record on the first play, he is likely to call in someone else for a second opinion or will play it again a day or two later, just to make sure. Your record has to get this sort of reception.

The independent plugger (and his company) becomes another member of the team working to put your record in the charts. Most pluggers now want to share in any success they create and over the last few years it has become normal for pluggers to ask for percentage points from the record they are promoting. The percentage runs from 0.5 to 2.5; one plugger even demands two points of the band's entire earnings over the next year! And he gets it.

The plugger is a vital part of the promotion machine and his skills can force that all-important lower chart entry and can go on to turn a heavily promoted record into a Top Five hit.

Pluggers and their assistants use every possible lever to secure air-play. They concentrate on Radio 1 and Radio 2 and the important local stations — Capital Radio, Radio London, Piccadilly Radio, Radio Forth, BRMB Radio, BBC Radio Bristol, Radio Clyde, etc. — and they usually know every important producer and DJ intimately.

The main currency used to 'buy' air-play is cocaine. For many pluggers and DJs (and quite a few producers) it is part of everyday life: the drug is regarded as the lubricant of the music business. But there is never a crude approach. There is never any suggestion in the form of 'You play this record for me and I'll give you a gramme'. What happens is that the plugger drops by, chats about the various new products he's working on and leaves a small plastic bag behind. It is discreet and non-specific. DJs and producers still have their right to reject a particular record, but the principle of the 'owed favour' is established.

The law of libel prevents those DJs, producers and stations involved in this exchange being named. By their nature such transactions are incredibly difficult to prove and, even if 'exposed' by such organs as the *News of the World* — human nature being what it is, the currency would merely change for a while.

The most obvious, yet 'acceptable,' bribe is the lunch. There's long been a saying that there is no such thing as a free lunch; this is clearly understood by both plugger and DJ/producer as they sip their Armagnacs. Some worthy DJs and producers insist on paying the bill after such meetings to ensure that they are under no obligation, but the majority do not.

Most pluggers will want to hear your record before deciding to take the project on. They need to make sure they are not being asked to promote something appalling. If they think the record has sufficient merit to protect their reputation they will agree a deal with you (once again, you are likely to pay for independent plugging out of your advance) which will involve weekly payments of between £400 and £1,500 plus an agreed percentage of the sales generated. The normal period of activity for a plugger is six to eight weeks. The plugger then swings into action and air play almost certainly follows.

TELEVISION

It is hard, but not impossible, to get booked for a TV slot. The main problem is that the shows most likely to take you are not likely to present you well and, as discussed in Chapter 1, many managements now choose not to take the risk, but to make videos available instead. These 'second league' TV shows include the lunch-time shows, 'Pebble Mill at One' and the ITV variations, and the children's shows.

You shouldn't turn your nose up at doing children's TV; a major part of your audience still hasn't kicked the habit of watching it and it can prove a very powerful promotion medium. The main drawback is the awful sets and sound.

The regulations about whether you may mime or not (always the preferred choice unless you are superb and very polished as a live act) differ from slot to slot and even from time to time within the slot. It all depends on the type of deal the show's producer, or the station's executives, have struck with the Musicians' Union. It is always worth asking if you can mime, but if you get a flat rejection you will have to take the decision whether or not to go ahead based on your own experience at playing live.

Some shows allow bands to pre-record back tracks in the TV studio before the taping of a broadcast, but insist that the vocals are sung live. Other shows want the entire performance live. Bear in mind that TV engineers aren't as concerned with sound quality as those engineers you will have met in the recording studio, and no matter what you do, you are bound to come out sounding weak.

This is another major reason why it is preferable to mime; you can be sure that the sound quality broadcast is identical to your record.

The lunch-time TV shows aren't likely to reach a high proportion of your target group (most of them will be at school), but there are enough unemployed or student viewers to make the exercise worthwhile (although they may not have much money available to spend on your record). You can always regard such appearances as training. It takes half a dozen TV appearances to get over the novelty of seeing yourself and begin to feel relaxed with the medium.

The best regional shows are the arts shows, such as BBC West's 'RPM'. The producers of these shows try to present the band in a sympathetic way and usually try to achieve the best sound possible within limited budgets.

Obviously, the most important are the networked shows such as those on Channel 4 and BBC 2. Programmes like Channel 4's 'The Tube' can be very influential. Trevor Horn spotted Frankie Goes To Hollywood's outrageous visual act on this show and awarded them their ZTT contract shortly afterwards. This type of show reaches a large proportion of your target audience and you shouldn't hesitate to appear if your plugger, manager or record label manages to get you a slot.

However, the ultimate showcase is BBC1's 'Top of the Pops', and everybody will be working to try and get you on it.

After a chequered past, BBC pop music programmes now seem to be free of corruption. The spotlight is on them to such an extent that every choice of act is analyzed both inside the BBC and the music business. Nearly all of the music which appears on 'Top of the Pops' is already in the charts, which protects the producers from any accusation of favouritism (while also putting incredible pressure on promoters to get a chart showing), but there are occasional slots for new acts and it is these the promoters work so hard to get.

The sound quality of 'Top of the Pops' — long the responsibility of that excellent sound engineer, Richard Chamberlain — is a lot better than on most TV shows. If you are invited to do the programme before your record is in the charts, it is almost like receiving a guarantee of having a hit. New bands are nearly always asked to perform in the studio for the invited audience (now supplemented by Equity members paid to seem interested) and whichever way the producer wants to record your track you can generally expect to get a sympathetic treatment.

Union and internal regulations prohibit 'Top of the Pops' showing more than a few videos in a half hour show, so making a video is not an automatic method of getting a showing on this most important of outlets. It can be of considerable help elsewhere, however.

THE VIDEO

Even though your record may be a priority for your record company, you may not make a promotional video to start with. The costs of producing a good video are so high — anywhere between £30,000 and £100,000 — that most record companies like to be sure that their touch hasn't failed them and that your record is beginning its climb up the charts before investing this kind of money.

Although it is rather chicken and egg — the arrival of the video certainly pushes a record up the charts — most records by new bands have to enter the Bottom 30 before a video is made.

How a pop video is made could fill a book on its own, but briefly, as you will be aware, your record is offered to several video production houses who prepare their ideas for illustrating your music in script and storyboard form. A storyboard is a series of small TV-like frames in which cartoonists draw the visual that the writers want to achieve.

How involved you get with the selection of the video theme depends on the autonomy you get in your deal, your interest in the topic and your time. If a video is being prepared while you are promoting the single up and down the country you just may not have time to consider how it is made.

Some bands just turn up on the first day of the shoot and do what they are told without having the slightest idea of the theme; some hardly appear in the videos made to promote their music: often just a few clips of their live performances will be intercut with the video images. Other bands virtually direct the video, coming up with the majority of creative ideas and playing a large role in the production. The structure is different on every occasion.

When a video is available to promote your record, you are likely to achieve much more regional and 'breakfast' TV airtime. Few British shows are content simply to play a video, however. Even if it were not for Musicians' Union regulations, most producers would also want the band in the studio, but the availability of an attractive video to improve the 'look' of a show is likely to win you more TV appearances.

HIT TIP

Despite the apparent 'success' of banned videos over the last few years, don't try to make a film which is likely to lose air time because of taste considerations. Despite brave faces and avowals to the contrary, the makers of most of those banned videos suffered very badly as a result of mishandling acceptability. In aiming to reach the limit of what is, and is not, acceptable, they misjudged the mood and were left with an expensive production which, at least in the UK, was worthless.

MARKETING

Your record will get into the charts primarily because of the marketing effort your record company puts behind you. Marketing is a word which now describes a multitude of sins and it has come to replace hype in the minds of most members of the music business. Hype is not respectable; marketing is.

THE PEOPLE WHO REALLY MATTER

While you're paying large amounts of money and giving away points to people like pluggers and producers, it is easy to overlook the most important people in the trade, the travelling salesmen. The majority are men, although there are a handful of saleswomen as well.

These reps are at the sharp end of the music business and collectively have the power to make a hit or to kill it. The most successful record companies pay attention to their reps and van salesmen and put a lot of trust in them. In return, the key salesmen are extremely well paid (more than you might expect) and are treated like kings inside their company.

Their official duties are to keep dealers informed about the company's products, to solicit orders, to supply stock and to ensure that the important outlets are properly supplied with the displays and merchandize which accompany priority records. For many, additional duties include bribing or 'influencing' dealers to take a specific product, and persuading dealers to log false sales whenever judicious.

The salesmen are told each week what their priorities are. Bonuses used to be paid to those who achieved specific sales targets, now most record companies prefer to link their bonuses to chart positions achieved. I have seen the chairman of one of Britain's largest record companies turn up at a distribution depot on a trading estate outside London on a cold Monday morning to brief his sales team. He told them precisely what positions he wanted to achieve for certain records in the charts that would be published ten days later. He told them in clear terms what the team of pluggers and publicists felt certain they could achieve in air-play and music paper coverage and gave his sales staff *carte blanche* to make the charts placings a reality. Every single-step increase up the chart ladder on two records earned each salesman an extra £20, in addition to that fat bonus already on offer if the chart target was achieved. Free products, tour jackets and other freebies to give dealers were distributed to the salesmen at that meeting and they went on their way to all corners of the British Isles.

YOUR ROLE IN MARKETING

You should try to do all you can to help the marketing of your record. Make an effort to go and meet the reps and sales staff: getting to know the faces behind the name on a record label will mean a lot to them, although it isn't a wonderful idea for *you* to start offering gold watches to the rep who sells most of your records. (It is a good idea, but the idea comes best from the sales managers).

HIT TIP

Sensible managers book as many gigs as possible for the first few weeks after a single is released and then keep the booking sheet empty. The reason is obvious: once a record starts to climb the charts, they want to be able to send the band wherever necessary to promote it and also to be available for the more lucrative gigs that are offered once the band is a chart name.

Some managers do take gigs beyond this cut-off point but add clauses to the booking contract which increase the band's fees according to the chart position achieved.

Before your single is released your management or agency office should have done its best to get you important gigs in different parts of the country to tie in with the sales activity around the single. If you're not a working band, most of the attention will have gone into getting TV and radio appearances.

Gigs are an important part of record promotion for several

reasons. The most obvious reason is that the public hear you and your single, but even if you played to a thousand people every night of the year, you still wouldn't be able to reach a number that was meaningful in promotional terms. What your gigs do is to give the sales reps something to sell against. If you've got a couple of dates in Leicester, the rep covering that area can give record dealers a reason for taking extra copies of your record. However, you must keep the sales staff informed of your movements. Many bands and even management offices (who should know better) forget this important facet of marking communication.

REACHING THE RECORD SHOPS

HIT TIP

If you feel nervous about walking into a record shop and introducing yourself, you should understand the way the business works. Those who are aren't able to promote themselves are unlikely to last long in the business.

Jonathan King has long been known as a superb self-promoter; when he has a record he wants to push he personally sits down and phones the key dealers around the country. Telephone sales are a useful back-up to in-field salesmen and you shouldn't hesitate to help your record along in any way that you can.

Your travels around the countryside also allow your publicist to arrange interviews for you with the local press and radio and, if you're lucky, spots on regional TV, which all influence dealers.

You can do a great deal of good by visiting record shops. You should ask your record label which are the most 'sensitive' shops and plan to visit them when you are gigging in their area. You are actually asking your label which are the chart shops and although you are unlikely to be handed a list of all 255, the locals reps will usually point you in the right direction, and will often accompany you on your visit to make the introductions.

REACHING THE PUBLIC

All your gigging, all the air-play and TV appearances and the advertising which appears in the consumer music press are supposedly aimed at the general public. In the early days, however, much of the activity is actually for the benefit of the record trade: your promoters are trying to hype the trade into believing you are actually reaching the public. This is unlikely to be the case, initially, but your activity and the marketing incentives should prompt the trade to stock your single and carry some point of sale display material. No one is quite sure when a record trips over from being heavily promoted to actually achieving genuine sales, but it does happen and sales slowly start to build.

One direct way of telling the public about your existence is fly-posting. If you've been on the road you'll already know all about this semi-illegal activity and you'll also know that petty criminals have got all the best sites in the major cities sewn up. Fly post without 'permission' in central London, Glasgow or Birmingham and within a few hours you'll inevitably receive a 'warning' from a burly moron who looks after the sites.

Many promotion companies think it is well worth paying the few hundred pounds a week it costs to use the underworld fly posting teams and if you are gigging locally to support a single it makes a lot of sense to advertise the gig alongside the single.

Direct advertising outside of the music press is very rarely used for a new act which is aiming at the singles charts. It might seem like common sense to you for a record company to buy TV commercials to promote your new single, but only a tiny proportion of the audience which would see the ads would be likely to buy your record. The teenagers who form the vast majority of the singles market are not regular TV watchers, they're usually out in the evenings avoiding their parents. For this reason a TV campaign would be incredibly wasteful and the money would be much better spent in media which reach your public directly.

Independent local radio would be a good medium for reaching singles buyers (at certain times of the day) were it not for the fact that there are various regulations which prevent local stations from taking record advertising. It is possible for record companies to advertise on ILR, but the restrictions on the amount of music which can be played during a commercial and the frequency with which such commercials appear do not make the package attractive. For this reason it is much better to concentrate efforts in a promotion company trying to procure in-programme air-play.

HIT TIP

The one exception to restricted radio advertising is Radio Luxembourg. The fortunes of 208 have suffered somewhat in recent years following the arrival of ILR and the pirates, but the station still commands good late night figures. If your record is considered right for this market, it may very well receive paid *exposé* on Radio Luxembourg.

Newspaper advertising suffers from the same problem as does TV and other general media: your market doesn't read papers enough to make advertising in them cost-effective. From this, it will be clear that it is very hard to reach people who buy single records simply by advertising. The more general album market is much easier to reach and you will have seen many TV ads trying to sell middle-of-the-road albums, especially by mail order. Newspaper and magazine ads also work in this market, but singles buyers are incredibly hard to reach.

Record companies do their best to reach this market, however, and have found one of the best outlets is to promote in the places where the record buyers go, the record shops and clubs. In-club promotion is mainly organized by the promotion companies, but it is the record companies who stage in-store competitions and other incentives to make the public aware of your records. These can be very effective and are just one more weapon in the vast armoury required to turn 'just another record' into a hit.

Finally we come to the very best form of publicity possible, word of mouth. If your band is any good, you'll generate this every time you play. No amount of producers, managers, record companies, pluggers or van salesmen can create this form by any means of 'hype' or 'priority' treatment. If you manage to generate this, you are on the way towards becoming a band which needs none of the machinations of the music business of the 1980s and you will go on to be a world-class act able to rely on your own talent alone.

The object of this book has not been to suggest that your talent is of no consequence; quite the opposite. In a situation where we are all manipulated in a media-dominated society, we need all of the freshness and originality available to us to combat the sterility of the packaged product. Although it may be useful for you to remember that you have to be packaged in order to fit the system, this book has been written in the hope that you cherish your individuality and that after the system has done its worst to you, you emerge as a major talent able to provide the world with the pleasure and entertainment it so desperately needs.

APPENDIX 1

UK RECORD COMPANIES

Ace Records, 132/134, Grafton Road, London NW5
Tel 01 267 5192
Action Replay Records, 12 Thayer Street, London W1M 5LD
Tel 01 935 8323
Air Records, 12 Stratford Place, London W1 Tel 01 408 2355
Albino Records, Studio 15, 98 Victoria Road, London NW10
Tel 01 965 0155
A & M Records, 136/140 New King's Road, London SW6 4LZ
Tel 01 736 3311
Amberlee Records, 387 Harrow Road, London W9
Tel 01 866 7748
Anagram Records, 53 Kensington Gardens Square, London W2
4BA Tel 01 727 0346
Antigua's Records, 16 Gorleston Road, London N15 5QR
Tel 01 809 6742
Arcade Records, 1/8 Stucley Place, London NW1 Tel 01 482 2211
Ariola/Arista Records, 3 Cavendish Square, London W1M 9HA
Tel 01 580 5566
Armageddon Records, 452 Fulham Road, London SW6 1BY
Tel 01 381 1393
Ark Records, 16 Benson Street, Liverpool 1 Tel 051 708 0193
Ash Records, Cropwell House, Salmon Lane, Kirkby in Ashfield,
Notts NG17 9HB, Tel 0623 752448
Attic Records, c/o Liaison & Promotion Co, 70 Gloucester Place,
London W1 Tel 01 935 5988
Aura Records, 1 Kendall Place, London W1H 3AG
Tel 01 486 5288
Automatic Records, 5 Avery Row, London W1X 9HA
Tel 01 493 9744

AVM Records, 30 Lingfield Road, London SW19 4PU
Tel 01 947 0191
BBJ International, 10/12 Carlisle Street, London W1V 5RF
Tel 01 734 4000
BeeBee Records, 59 Marlpit Lane, Coulsdon, Surrey CR3 2HF
Tel 01 486 9531
Beggars Banquet Records, 17/19 Alma Road, London SW18
Tel 01 870 9912
Big Boy Records, 5 Dorlcote Road, London SW18 Tel 01 870 1683
Black & White Records, 31 D'Arblay Street, London W1V 4LR
Tel 01 434 4179
Black Eye Music, Tower Cottages, Whaddon Road, Mursley,
Milton Keynes, Bucks Tel 0296 72584
Blaze Records, 14 New Burlington Street, London W1X 2LA
Tel 01 734 3251
Blue Ocean Records, 7 Hale Lane, London NW7
Tel 01 892 6882/346 2727
Boadicea Record Company, 10 Green Street, London W1
Tel 01 493 4178
Breakaway Records, 18/19 Warwick Street, London W1R 5RB
Tel 01 434 1495/6
Brent Black Music Co-op, 383 High Road, London NW10
Tel 01 451 4545
Bright Records, 34/36 Maddox Street, London W1R 9PD
Tel 01 408 0288
Broadside Records, Studley House, 68A Limes Road, Tettenhall,
Wolverhampton Tel 0902 753047
Broken Records, Regent House, 235/241 Regent Street,
London W1A 2JT Tel 01 493 1610
Bronze Records, 100 Chalk Farm Road, London NW1 8EH
Tel 01 267 4499
Buffalo Records, 10 St Mary's Hill, Stamford Tel 0780 51736
Bullseye Records, Air House, Spennymoor, Co. Durham
Tel 0388 814632

Burning Rome Records, 25 Denmark Street, London WC2
Tel 01 240 7443
Butt Records, 32 Avon Trading Estate, Avonmore Road, London W14 8TS Tel 01 603 6831
Cadillac Music, 180 Shaftesbury Avenue, London WC2H 8SJ
Tel 01 838 3048/340 3933
CBS Records, 17/19 Soho Square, London W1V 6HE
Tel 01 734 8181
Challenge Records, 262 Holloway Road, London N7
Tel 01 609 7017/8
Champion Records, 23 Powis Gardens, London NW11 8HH
Tel 01 455 2469
Chandos Records, 41 Charing Cross Road, London WC2H 0AR
Tel 01 437 1448/5512
Channel Records, Crofton House, 1 New Cavendish Street, London W1M 7RP Tel 01 935 8970
Chantel Records, 3A Ashfield Parade, London N14 5EH
Tel 01 886 6236
Charisma Records, 90 Wardour Street, London W1
Tel 01 434 1351
Charly Records, 156/166 Ilderton Road, London SE15 1NT
Tel 01 639 8603/4/5/6
China Disques, 176A Queenstown Road, London SW8
Tel 01 675 4498/720 4884
Chiswick Records, 132/134 Grafton Road, London NW5
Tel 01 267 5192
Chorale Music, 29 Paddington Street, London W1H 3RG
Tel 01 486 2362
Chrysalis Records, 12 Stratford Place, London W1
Tel 01 408 2355
Circle In The Square Records, 49 Derby Street, Kelvingrove, Glasgow Tel 041 334 5099
City Records, The Charterhouse, Eltringham Street, London SW18
Tel 01 874 5868

Coast Records, The Music Works Studios, 23 Benwell Road, London N7 Tel 01 609 1377
Coda Records, 17/19 Alma Road, London SW18 Tel 01 870 9912
Control Music, 48 Portland Place, London W1N 3DG Tel 01 323 4743
Cow Pie Records, 40 Meadowcroft Road, London N13 4EQ Tel 01 882 6378
Crazy Viking Music Co, 6 Heath Close, London W5 Tel 01 991 0993
Criminal Damage Records, 91 Swansea Road, Reading RG1 8HA Tel 0734 23339
CSA Records, 101 Chamberlayne Road, London NW10 3NP Tel 01 960 8466
Cube Records, 19/20 Poland Street, London W1V 3DD Tel 01 734 8121
Da Doo Ron Ron Records, 116 Churchgate, Southport, Merseyside PR9 7JE Tel 0704 212505
Dakota Records, 14A Shouldham Street, London W1 Tel 01 723 1063
The Dance Network, 49 Bruce Grove, London N17 6RN Tel 01 808 9385
Dancing Sideways Records, 116 Tufnell Park Road, London N7 Tel 01 263 6587
Dead Badger Records, 17/19 Alma Road, London SW18 Tel 01 370 6175
Dead Hedgehog Enterprises, 20 St John's Road, Watford, Hertfordshire WD1 1QA Tel 0923 52442
Dead Horse Records, 50 South Park Terrace, Ilford, Essex Tel 01 478 4150
Death Records, P.O. Box 489 London SE10 9DY Tel 01 305 0662
Decca Records (UK), 50 New Bond Street, London W1 Tel 01 491 7600
DEP International, 92 Fazelet Street, Birmingham Tel 021 6431321

Desire Records, 46A Montagu Square, London W1
Tel 01 723 9269
Devil Records, 6 Myra Avenue, Morecambe, Lancs LA4 5SG
Tel 0524 424586
Dingle's Records, 322 Whitchurch Lane, Edgware, Middlesex HA8 6QX Tel 01 951 0846
Diversion Records, 59 Paddocks Mead, Woking, Surrey GU21 3QP
Tel 048 67 81364
DJM Records, James House, 5 Theobald's Road, London WC1X 8SE Tel 01 242 6886
Do It Records, 81 Harley House, Marylebone Road, London NW1
Tel 01 486 3602/8855
Ear & Eye Production Co, 3 Headingley Mount, Headingley, Leeds, W. Yorks LS6 3EL Tel 0532 741431
Earthworks, 162 Oxford Gardens, London W10 Tel 01 969 5145
Ebony Records, 18 Mayfield Street, Hull HU3 1NS
Tel 0482 25850
E G Records, 63A Kings Road, Chelsea, London SW3 4NT
Tel 01 730 2162
Elecstar, 30 Lingfield Road, London SW19 4PU
Tel 01 947 0191/0149
Electric Bubblegum Records, c/o 21 Heelis Street, Barnsley, S. Yorks Tel 0226 41847
EMI Records (Ireland), 130 Slaney Road, Dublin Industrial Estate, Dublin II Tel 309077
EMI Records (UK), EMI House, 20 Manchester Square, London W1A 1ES Tel 01 486 4488
Ensign Records, 3 Monmouth Place, London W2 Tel 01 727 0527
ERC Records, 46 South Molton Street, London W1
Tel 01 409 3122
ESO Records, 36 Goulden Road, Manchester 20 Tel 061 806 6420
Esoteric Records, 33 Barberry House, Shannon Road, Kings Norton, Birmingham Tel 021 458 7503
ESSP (Electric Synthesizer, Sound Projects), The Sound House, P.O. Box 37B, East Molesey, Surrey KT8 9JB Tel 01 979 9997

Red Bus House, 48 Broadley Terrace, London NW1
Tel 01 258 0324
Factory Records, 86 Palatine Road, Didsbury, Manchester 20
Tel 061 434 3876
Fast Product, 21 Atholl Crescent, Edinburgh EH3 8HQ
Tel 031 229 8946
Fatal Records, 106 Tollington Park, London N4
Tel 01 434 3035/6
Fat Hen Records, Hillhouse, Netherfield Hill, Battle, Sussex TN33 0LQ Tel 04246 3641
Faulty Productions, 194/196 Kensington Park Road, London W11
Tel 01 727 0734/221 4566
Fearless Productions, 51 Gas Street, Birmingham B1 2JX
Tel 021 643 4016/4570
Feelgood Records, 14 New Burlington Street, London W1X 2LR
Tel 01 734 3251
Fetish Records, 40 Denbigh Street, London SW1 Tel 01 828 1978
Flicknife Records, 82 Adelaide Grove, London W12
Tel 01 743 9412
Flip Records, 9 Carnaby Street, London W1V 1PG
Tel 01 437 3852/1958
The Flying Record Company, 1 Lower James Street, London W1R 3PN Tel 01 439 3638
Focus Records, Focus Studios, Vine Yard, Sanctuary Street, London SE1 Tel 01 403 1202
Geoff's Records, 10 Royal London Estate, West Road, London N17
Tel 01 808 5301
Ghetto Music, 4 Denmark Street, London WC2H 8LP
Tel 01 242 2250
Glass Records, 79 Wellesley Court, London W9 1RG
Tel 01 289 3108
Global Records, 38 Biddulph Mansions, Biddulph Road, London W9 1HX Tel 01 289 6337
Go Ahead Records, Kerchesters, Waterhouse Lane, Kingswood, Surrey Tel 0737 832837

Goat Bag Records & Music, 7 Nesbit Close, London SE3 0XB
Tel 01 318 7389
Go! Discs, Go! Mansions, 8 Wendell Road, London W12
Tel 01 743 3845/3919
Goldbar Records, Vogue House, 1 Hanover Square, London W1
Tel 01673 8974
Golden Sounds, 15 Old Barn Close, Gnosall, Staffs ST20 0DY
Tel 0785 823348
Goldfish Records, 37 Pointout Road, Bassett,
Southampton SO1 7DL Tel 0703 768325
Goughsound, 32 Avon Trading Estate, Avonmore Road,
London W14 8TS Tel 01 603 6831
Graduate Records, Chaddesley House, 196 Wolverhampton Street,
Dudley, W. Midlands Tel 0384 59048/21159
Gull Records, 59A Connaught Street, London W2
Tel 01 402 1362
Hannibal Records, 3 Logan Place, London W8 6QN
Tel 01 370 6166
Hansa Productions, 26 Castlereagh Street, London W1
Tel 01 402 2191
Harbor Records, 16 Hampstead Gardens, London NW11 7EU
Tel 01 458 3436
Heavy Metal, 165 Wolverhampton Road, Sedgley DY3 1QR
Tel 0902 345345
Helios Records, 28 Dalrymple Crescent, Edinburgh EH9 2NX
Tel 031 667 3633
Hengis Records, 33 St George Road, London N13 4AT
Tel 01 882 4797
Hertford Records, 38 Hertford Street, London W1Y 8BA
Tel 01 493 5961
High Energy Records, 62 Rowley Street, Stafford Tel 0785 211172
Hit The Spot Records, 19 Woodfield Road, London W9
Tel 01 286 3043
Hollywood Records, 38/40 Upper Clapton Road, London E5 8BG
Tel 01 806 0071/4

Hot Lead Records, 2 Laurel Bank, Golcar, Huddersfield, Yorks HD7 4ER Tel 0484 846333

Ice Records, P.O. Box 212. London SW1 Tel 01 730 7291

Indipop Records, 92 Birbeck Road, Enfield, Middlesex Tel 01 366 7023

Inferno Records, 3 Dale End, Birmingham B4 7LN Tel 021 236 5493

Initial Records, 36/38 Hanway Street, London W1P 9DE Tel 01 637 2698

In Phaze Records, 737 Eastern Avenue, Newbury Park, Ilford, Essex Tel 01 597 2776

IOU Records, 19 Woodfield Road, London W9 Tel 01 286 3043

Ironic Records, P.O. Box 58 Wokingham, Berks RG11 7HN Tel 0344 772061

Island Records, 22 St Peter's Square, London W6 Tel 01 741 1511

It's Magic Records, 6 West Hampstead Mews, London NW6 Tel 01 940 5088

Jasmine Records, 29 Bell Street, London NW1 5BY Tel 01 723 1102/3

JDS Records, 11 Connaught Place, London W2 2ET Tel 01 402 9463

Jeap Records, The Studio Complex, 45 Victoria Road, Romford, Essex RM1 2JH Tel 0708 27641

Jet Records, 35 Portland Place, London W1N 3AG Tel 01 637 2111

Jive Records, Zomba House, 165/167 Willesden High Road, London NW10 3SG Tel 01 459 8899

JSP Records, 112 Sunny Gardens Road, London NW4 Tel 01 203 1324

Jungle Records, 24 Gaskin Street, London N1 Tel 01 359 8444/9161

K A Records, 9 Paddington Street, London W1 Tel 01 935 1247/486 7647

Kay-Drum Records, 42 Priory Avenue, Bedford Park, London W4 1TY Tel 01 995 7470

Kilo Music, 620 Western Avenue, London W3 0TU
Tel 01 992 8055

Kin'Ell Records, 150 Southampton Row, London WC1
Tel 01 278 3331

Kingdom Records, 9/11 Monmouth Street, London WC2 9DA
Tel 01 836 4763

Klub Records, 9 Watt Road, Hillington Industrial Estate, Hillington, Glasgow G52 4RY Tel 041 882 9060

K R Recordings, P.0. Box 212, London SW1 Tel 01 730 7291

Le Beat Route Records, 2 Princes Street, London W1
Tel 01 499 7151

Logo Records, 52 Red Lion Street, London WC1 Tel 01 242 9397

Magnet Records, Magnet House, 22 York Street, London W1H 4FD Tel 01 486 8151

Magnum Music Group, Coronation Suite, Shepperton Studio Centre, Shepperton, Middlesex, TW19 0QD Tel 09328 60363

Mainspring Records, 2 Darby Crescent, Sunbury-on-Thames, Middlesex Tel 09327 82358

Major Record Company, 13 Numa Court, Brentford Marina, Brentford, Middlesex Tel 01 560 6090

Malaco Records, 89 Marylebone High Street, London W1
Tel 01 487 2660

Management Agency & Music, 24/25 New Bond Street, London W1 Tel 01 629 9255

Marathon Records, 30 Great Portland Street, London W10
Tel 01 637 2256/3067

Marco Music (Productions), P.O. Box 212, London SW1
Tel 01 730 7291

Mawson & Wareham (Music), 11 Blackett Street, Newcastle-upon-Tyne, NE1 5BS Tel 0632 326461

May Day Records, 11 Davies Street, Liverpool L16 6HB
Tel 051 236 0989

Mays Records, 11 Oxford Circus Avenue, Oxford Circus, London W1 Tel 01 439 2568

MCA Records, 1 Gt Pulteney Street, London W1R 3FW
Tel 01 439 9951

MDM Communications, 28A High Street, West Wickham,
Kent BR4 0NJ Tel 01 777 0811

The Mega Organisation, 9/10 Bridge Street, York Y01 1DD
Tel 0904 55584

Megastar, Spirella Building, Bridge Road, Letchworth, Herts
Tel 046 267 9361

Mellow McKenzie Records, 155 Chiswick Village,
London W4 3DG Tel 01 994 3803

Meridian Records, P.O. Box 317, London SE9 4SF
Tel 01 857 3213

Micrometro, Zomba House, 165/167 High Road, London
NW10 2SG Tel 01 459 8899

Midnight Music (Records), P.O. Box 333 Bushey,
Watford WD2 3UN Tel 01 950 9507

Miles Ahead Records, 4 Rising Sun Cottages, Forest Green,
Holyport, Berks SL6 2NE Tel 0628 39790

Mix Records, 85 Tottenham Lane, London N8 9BE
Tel 01 348 1903/0455

MMC Recordings, 3 Park Cottages, Green Lane, Stanmore,
Middlesex Tel 01 954 0689

Moggie Records, 101 Hazelwood Lane, London N13 5HQ
Tel 01 886 2801

Monarch Records, Sheepcote Farm House, Sheepcote Lane,
Orpington, Kent Tel 66 25189/20901

Montmusic, Sandridgebury Court, Sandridgebury Lane,
Sandridgebury, St Albans, Herts AL3 6JB Tel 0727 56806

Moon Records, 10 Southborough Road, Surbiton, Surrey KT6 6JN
Tel 01 390 2757

Motown Records, 16 Curzon Street, London W1Y 7FF
Tel 01 493 1603

MRP, 75 Woodpark Drive, Knaresborough, N. Yorks HG5 9DL
Tel 0423 863776

Multicord, 1 & 3 Ravensworth View, Dunston,
Tyne & Wear NE11 9DQ Tel 0632 609209
Mute Records, 49/53 Kensington, Gardens Square, London W2
Tel 01 221 4840
MVM Records, P.O. Box 118, Sheffield S10 1DW
Tel 0742 308667/01 788 5162
Namedrop Records, c/o Rough Trade Records,
Nancy Boys Music, 56 Wigmore Street, London W1
Tel 01 486 5745
NB Records, c/o ETC 56 Palace Records, London N8
Tel 01 341 0144
Neat Records (DWE), 71 High Street, East Wallsend,
Tyne & Wear NE28 7RJ Tel 0632 624999
Nectar Music, Erawan House P.O. Box 18, Chertsey,
Surrey KT16 0LX Tel 093287 3151
Neon Records, P.O. Box 459, Lawton Road, Alsager, Stoke-on-Trent ST7 2EU Tel 0782 09363 5029
Neovox Record Company, 14 Regent Road, Harborne,
Birmingham 17 Tel 021 426 3663
Nervous Records, 4-36 Dabbs Hill Lane, Northolt, Middlesex
Tel 01 422 3462
New Leaf Records, 9 Church Road, Conington, Peterborough
PE7 3QJ Tel 0487 830701
New Music Enterprises, 46 Alexandra Crescent, Bromley,
Kent BR1 4EU Tel 01 460 6584
The Next Road Company, 6 Holyoake Walk, London N2
Tel 01 883 4137
Nimbus Records, Wyastone Leys, Monmouth, Gwent NP5 3SR
Tel 0600 890682
Nite-Life, 132 Grafton Road, London NW5 Tel 01 267 5192
No Future Records, 3 Adelaide House, 21 Wells Road, Malvern,
Worcsestershire WR14 2RH Tel 06845 65319/68036
Northeast Music, 6 Mendip Close, Peterlee,
County Durham SR8 2JL Tel 0783 871508

Oily Records, 6 Cedar Place, Aberdeen AB2 3SZ
Tel 0224 632749/630120
101 Records International, 25 Lexington Street, London W1R 3HQ
Tel 01 437 5175/6363
Only A Revolution, P.O. Box 337, London W5 4XG
Tel 01 847 2625
Orchid Music, Unit K5, Field Way, Greenford Industrial Estate, Greenford, Middlesex Tel 01 575 7117
Organic Records, 79 Kingshill, Brandon Street, London SE17 1UH
Tel 01 703 2777
Oryx Recordings, South Snowdon Quay, Portmadoc LL49 9ND
Tel 0766 2877
Osceola Records, 36 Bloemfontein Road, London W12
Tel 01 743 0427
Outlet Homespun, Recording Co., Outlet House, 48 Smithfield Square, West Belfast Tel 0232 222826
Out To Lunch Records, 21 Argyll Mansions, 303/323 Kings Road, London SW3 5ER Tel 01 351 1654
Oval Records, 11 Liston Road, London SW4 Tel 01 622 0111
Overdrive Records, White Horse Cottage, Wotton Road, Iron Acton, Bristol BS17 1XQ Tel 0272 277547
Pacific Records, 51 Islip Street, London NW5 Tel 01 267 2917/8
Page One Records, 29 Ruston Mews, London W11 1RB
Tel 01 221 7179/7381
Paladin Records, 12 Berwick Street, London W1 Tel 01 437 4844
Panache Music, 362 York Road, London SW18 1SP
Tel 01 870 8522
Papier Mache Records, 19 Studdridge Street, London SW6
Tel 01 736 0810
Parasol Records, Suite 421, Warehouse 0, Metropolitan Wharf, Wapping Mall, London E1 Tel 01 488 4880
Passion Records, Southbank House, Black Prince Road, London SE1 7SJ Tel 01 735 8171
Pastafont Music, 22 Hambledon Hill, Epsom, Surrey KT18 7BZ
Tel 03727 41022/22202

Pavilion Records, 48 High Street, Pembury, Kent TN2 4NU
Tel 089282 2042
Peak Records, 58 Avenue Road, Harold Wood, Romford, Essex
Tel 0708 73200
Peninsula Records, 37 Brook Street, Driffield, E. Yorks YO25 7QP
Tel 0377 47311/47191
Perfect Records, Osborn House, 9/13 Osborn Street,
London E1 6TD Tel 01 247 1311
Phonogram Records, 50 New Bond Street, London W1Y 9HA
Tel 01 491 4600
Pilgrim Records, 3 Beggarwood Lane, Basingstoke,
Hants RG23 7LP Tel 0256 59211
Pip Records, 29 North End Road, Golders Green, London NW11
Tel 01 455 4707
Plankton Records, 236 Sebert Road, London E7 0NP
Tel 01 534 8500
Plaza Records, 126 Hampstead Way, London NW11
Tel 01 455 7965
Plezure Records, 33 Parkway, London NW1 Tel 01 482 1723
Polo Records, 23 Powis Gardens, London NW11 8HH
Tel 01 455 2469
Polydor, 13/14 Saint George Street, London W1R 9DE
Tel 01 499 8686
PolyGram Leisure, 15 Saint George Street, London W1R 9DE
Tel 01 499 0422
Posh Records, 11A Victoria Square, Holmfirth, Huddersfield,
Tel 0484 682255
Powerstation Records, 38 Coney Street, York Tel 0904 642451
Precious Records, 19 Acre Lane, London SW2 Tel 01 274 0164
President Records, Broadmead House, 21 Panton Street,
London SW1Y 4DR Tel 01 839 4672/5
Press Color Records, 47 St John's Road, Stansted, Essex
Tel 0279 81 2864
Priority Records, 90 Boston Place, London NW1 Tel 01 724 0907

The Production League, 4 Auckland Court, London SE27 9PE
Tel 01 761 0178
Proto Record Company, 7 Kentish Town Road, London NW1
8NH Tel 01 482 3306
PRT Records, ACC House, 17 Great Cumberland Place,
London W1A 1AG Tel 01 262 8040
Public Recordings, 51 Gas Street, Birmingham B1 2JX
Tel 021 643 4489
Purple Records, 25 Newman Street, London W1P 3HA
Tel 01 323 1272/5
PVA Recordings, Alpha Tower, Paradise Circus,
Birmingham B1 1TT Tel 021 643 4011
PVK Productions, Stewart House, Hillbottom Road, Sands Estate,
High Wycombe, Bucks Tel 0494 36401
Quiet Records, The Metrostore, 231 The Vale, London W3 7QS
Tel 01 740 0680
Radialchoice, 17 Nelson Road, London SE10 Tel 01 853 5899
Radioactive Records, 49 Greek Street, London W1
Tel 01 437 7418
Radio Records, 24 Furze Street, London E3 Tel 01 987 1681
RAK Records, 42/48 Charlbert Street, London NW8 7BU
Tel 01 586 2012
RAM Records, Number 4, 10 Queens Road, Twickenham
TW1 4ES Tel 01 891 3146
Rascal Records, 1/3 Hill Rise, Richmond, Surrey Tel 01 940 5283
Rat Race Records, 10A Belmont Street, London NW1
Razor Records, 52 Red Lion Street, London WC1 Tel 01 242 9397
R & B Records, Red Bus House, 48 Broadley Terrace, London
NW1 Tel 01 258 0324
RCA Record Division, 1 Bedford Avenue, London WC1B 3DT
Tel 01 636 8311
Rebecca Records, 17 Kingsway, Mortlake, London SW14
Tel 01 876 8509

Recommended Records, 387 Wandsworth Road, London SW8
Tel 01 622 8834

Record Shack Records, 12 Berwick Street, London W1
Tel 01 437 3655

Red Flame, The Metrostore, 231 The Vale, London W3 7QS
Tel 01 743 0006/8

Red Lightnin' Records, The White House, North Lopham, Diss, Norfolk Tel 0379 88 693

Rel Records, 7A Atholl Place, Edinburgh EH3 8HP
Tel 031 229 9651

Remote Records, c/o 6/8 Alie Street, London E1 8DE
Tel 01 481 9917

RGH Records, 12 Trundle Street, London SE1 1QT
Tel 01 403 4929

Rhythmic Records, 50 Ernest Road, Wivenhoe, Essex CO7 9LQ
Tel 0206 222328

Rialto Records, 4 Yeoman's Row, London SW3 2AH
Tel 01 584 2441

Riddle Records, 15 Great Western Road, London W9
Tel 01 289 1021

Rising Records, Victoria Chambers, 30/32 London Road, Sheffield S2 4LH Tel 0742 28264/5

Ritz Music Company, 8/21 Fitzjohn's Avenue, London NW3 5JY
Tel 01 435 5279

Ritz Records (UK), Regent House, 235/241 Regent Street, London W1A 2JT Tel 01 493 1610

Riva Records, 2 New Kings Road, London SW6 Tel 01 731 4131

R & R Records, Highfield House, Kenyon Lane, Culcheth, Cheshire WA3 4AX Tel 092576 5021

Robin Records, P.O. Box 3, Hessle, N. Humberside
Tel 0482 649193

Rocket Records, 125 Kensington High Street, London W8 5SN
Tel 01 938 1741

Rock Shop Records, Portsmouth, Tel 0705 81734

Rock Steady Records, 8 Higher Road, Urmston, Manchester 31
Tel 061 748 2198
Rogue Records, 2 Eastdale, East Street, Farnham, Surrey GU9 7TB
Tel 0252 724638
Rola Music, Norfolk House, Well Walk, Cheltenham,
Gloucestershire Tel 0242 38543/41147
Rollercoaster Records, P.O. Box 18F, Chessington,
Surrey KT9 1UZ Tel 01 397 8957
Rooster Records, 33 Park Chase, Wembley, Middlesex HA9 8EQ
Tel 01 902 5523/2024
Rose Records, The Priory, Haywards Heath, Sussex
Tel 0444 412284
Ross Records, 29 Main Street, Turriff, Aberdeenshire
Tel 0888 62403
Rotate Records, 17 Station Street, London SE25 5AH
Tel 01 771 5777/8
Rough Trade Records, 137 Blenheim Crescent, London W11
Tel 01 221 1100
RSO Records, 10 Nottingham Place, London W1M 3FA
Tel 01 487 5001
Runaway Records, 38 North Row, London W1 Tel 01 499 2014
Rundown Records, 15A Temple Road, Canterbury, Kent
Tel 0227 60691
Rutland Records, 71 Rutland Road, Chesterfield,
Derbyshire S40 1ND Tel 0246 79976
Satril Records, Satril House, 444 Finchley Road,
London NW2 2HY Tel 01 435 8063
Saydisc Records, The Barton, Inglestone Common, Badminton,
Gloucestershire Tel 045 424 266
Seeing Red Records, 32 Stanley Road, Brighton
Tel 0273 692960/27845
77 Records, 21 Tower Street, London WC2H 9NS
Tel 01 240 1354
Shark Records, 23 Rolls Court Avenue, London SE24
Tel 01 737 4580

Shoc-wave Records, Garden Flat, 17 Belmont Road, St Andrews, Bristol BS6 Tel 0272 46443
Silver Lining Records, 22 Shardeloes, Old Amersham, Bucks HP7 0RL Tel 02403 28166
Sin City Records, 22A Forest Road West, Nottingham NG7 4EQ Tel 0602 784714/708622
Sinister Productions, 138 Park Lane, London W1 Tel 01 493 8366
Skeleton Records, 94 Argyle Street, Birkenhead, Merseyside Tel 051 647 9650/4505
Slipped Discs, The Showroom, 307/309 Goldhawk Road, London W12 8EZ Tel 01 748 1319
Society Records, 17 Gosfield Street, London W1P 7HE Tel 01 631 5221
Solida Leisure & Entertainment Group, 5 Robertson House, Tooting Grove, London SW17 Tel 01 672 4566
Solid Gold Records, 14 New Burlington Street, London W1X 2LR Tel 01 734 3251
Solid Records, Mill Cottage, Brimpton, Nr Reading, Berks Tel 073521 3844
Solomonic Production, 23 Turnpike Lane, London N8 Tel 01 341 4355
Solo Records, 31 Gladstone Street, Southwark, London SE1 6EY Tel 01 928 4274
Some Bizzare Label, 17 St Annes Court, London W1 Tel 01 734 9901
Someone Else's Music, 34B Beresford Road, London N5 Tel 01 359 5242
Sound Advice, 30 Lingfield Road, London SW19 4PU Tel 01 947 4767/0149
Sounds Intimate, 4 Queen Street, Horsham, West Sussex RH13 5AQ Tel 0403 67038
Sour Grape, 82 Pathfield Road, London SW16 Tel 01 677 0948
Southern Records, c/o Keith Evans & Co, 56 Wigmore Street, London W1 Tel 01 486 5745

Spartan Records, London Road, Wembley, Middlesex
Tel 01 903 4753
Spectacle Productions, 90 Croxted Road, West Dulwich, London SE21 8NP Tel 0908 313313
Speed Records, 12 Thayer Street, London W1M 5LD
Tel 01 935 8323
Spellbound Records, Southbank House, Black Prince Road, London SE1 7SJ Tel 01 735 8171/587 1545
Sphinx Records, 7 Huston Terrace, Purfleet, Essex
Tel 04026 2489
Spider Records, 101 Torridge Road, Sutton Lane Estate, Langley, Berks Tel 0753 40444
Spinach Records, 8 Nursery Road, Prestwich, Manchester M25 7DN Tel 061 773 8914
Spindriff Records, 6/8 Alie Street, London E1 8DE
Tel 01 481 9917
Spirit Records, Fulmer Gardens House, Fulmer, Bucks SL3 6HF
Tel 02816 2143/2109
Spitfire Records, Carlton Tower Place, Sloane Street, London SW1X 9PZ Tel 01 235 0168
Spiv Records, 24 Devonshire Road, Liverpool 8 Tel 051 709 9460
Splash Records, 38 North Row, London W1R 1DH
Tel 01 409 0287
Spring Records, 24 Old Burlington Street, London W1X 1RL
Tel 01 434 2973
Springsong Records, 24 Old Burlington Street, London W1
Tel 01 434 2973
Springtime Records, The Basement, Norfolk Mansions, Lithos Road, London NW3 Tel 01 435 1166
Squeaky Shoes Records, 387 Wandsworth Road, London SW8
Tel 01 720 0170
Stage One (Records), Parshire House, 2 Kings Road, Haslemere, Surrey GU27 2QA Tel 0428 4001
Stagmanor Records, 6 Heathview Road, Thornton Heath, Croydon Surrey CR4 7PL Tel 01 684 9439

Stairway Records, 30 Hilldown Road, Streatham, London SW16 3DZ Tel 01 679 2853

Stallion Records, 76 Roebuck House, Stag Place, London SW1 Tel 01 828 0227

Starblend, 30 Lingfield Road, London SW19 4PU Tel 01 947 4767/0149

Star Track Recording Co, 353A Church Road, London E10 Tel 01 558 5549

State Records, 26/27 Castlereagh Street, London W1 Tel 01 402 2191

Statik Records, 1A Normand Gardens, Greyhound Road, London W14 Tel 01 381 0116/385 0567

Steinar Records (UK), IBC House, 1/3 Mortimer Street, London W1 Tel 01 637 5277

Stiff Records, 115/123 Bayham Street, London NW1 Tel 01 485 5622

Stiletto Records, 122 Holland Park Avenue, London W11 4UA Tel 01 229 3221

Street Sounds, Streetwave House, 2/4 Queens Drive, London W3 0HA Tel 01 992 9077

Street Tunes, Flat 45, Barrington Court, Muswell Hill, London N10 Tel 01 883 0775

Streetwave Records, Streetwave House, 2/4 Queens Drive London W3 0HA Tel 01 993 1512

Strike Records, P.O. Box 396, London W11 2LZ Tel 01 323 1272/5

Sunburst Records, 25 Newman Street, London W1P 3HA Tel 01 323 1272/5

Supermusic, 9/10 Bridge Street, York YO1 1DD Tel 0904 55584

Survival Records, P.O. Box 337, London W5 4XG Tel 01 847 2625

SUS, 10 Albion Way, London SE13, Tel 01 852 8880

Swamp Records, 6 Chieveley Mews, London Road, Sunningdale, Berks SL5 0UD Tel 0990 26425 & 20342

Sylvantone Records, 17 Allerton Grange Way, Leeds LS17 6LP
Tel 0532 687788
Tabitha Records, 38 Cordery Road, Exeter EX2 9DJ
Tel 0392 79914
Tangent Records, 50 Stroud Green Road, London N4 3EF
Tel 01 263 6403
Tao Dance, 49 Harborne Park Road, Birmingham B17 0DE
Tel 021 427 8473
Target Records, 8/9 Giltspur Street, London EC1A 9DE
Tel 01 236 5940
Teddy Bear Records, 9A Park Parade, London NW10
Tel 01 965 7600
Teesbeat Records, 10 South Road, Norton-on-Tees, Cleveland
Tel 0642 552493
Telstar Records, 21 Napier Place, London W14 8LG
Tel 01 602 8433
Temple Records, Shillinghill, Temple, Midlothian, Scotland
Tel 087530 328
10 Records, 101/109 Ladbroke Grove, London W11
Tel 01 229 1282
Tent Records, 147 Gorseway, Rush Green, Romford, Essex
RM7 0SA Tel 01 375 1881
Thaw Records, 44 Roderick Road, London NW3 Tel 01 482 0536
Sydney Thompson Records, Eastcote Point, Cuckoo Hill, Pinner,
Middlesex HA5 2AL Tel 01 886 8310
Threshold Records, 53-55 High Street, Cobham, Surrey
KT11 3DP Tel 01 266 4142
Tidal Wave Records, 19 Woodfield Road, London W9
Tel 01 286 3043
Topic Records, 50 Stroud Green Road, London N4 3EF
Tel 01 263 6403
Towerbell, 32/34 Gondar Gardens, London NW6 1HG
Tel 01 431 2770
Trial Records, Mondice High Street, Acton, Sudbury, Suffolk
Tel 0787 77317/73126

Triumphant Records, 40 Queens Gardens, London W2 3AA
Tel 01 402 7581
Trojan Records, 326 Kensal Road, London W10 5BL
Tel 01 969 6651
Troll Kitchen, 6 Staplands Road, Broadgreen, Liverpool L14 3LL
Tel 051 259 4503/051 263 5734
12 St Records, 1 St Albans Road, Kingston, Surrey
Tel 01 549 9181
Two Ten Records, P.O. Box 210 Watford, Herts WD2 4YG
Tel 0923 34146
T W Records, Unit 4, Lysander Road, Bowerhill, Melksham, Wilts
Tel 0225 707799
Unlikely Records, 42 Haven Close, Felixstowe, Suffolk IP11 8LF
Tel 0394 286286
Upright Records, 49-53 Kensington, Gardens Square, London W8
Tel 01 229 8856
Utopia Records, Utopia Village, 7 Chalcot Road,
London NW1 8LH Tel 01 586 3434
Valentine Music Group, 7 Garrick Street, London WC2E 9AR
Tel 01 240 1628/9
Virgin Records, 2/4 Vernon Yard, 119 Portobello Road,
London W11 2DX Tel 01 727 8070
Vista Records, P.O. Box 144, Cambridge CB2 5QA
Tel 0223 870574
Vista Sounds, 25 Park Way Edgware, Middlesex HA8 5EX
Tel 01 951 3177/952 2776
Vita Viva Sound, The Cottage, Reading Road, Lower Basildon,
Reading RG8 9NL Tel 049162 789
VJM Records/Halcyon Records, 12 Slough Lane, Kinsbury,
London NW9 8QL Tel 01 205 2587
VM Records, High Street, Cumnor, Oxford OX2 9QD
Tel 0685 863566
Vox Productions (GB), 11 Elgood House, Wellington Road,
London NW8 9TG Tel 01 722 1208

Vroom Records, 90/92 Queens Road, Watford, Herts
Tel 0923 40294
Waiting-in-Vain Records, 42 Park View Road, London NW10 1AL
Tel 01 450 5987
Waterfront Music, 74 High Street, Old Town, Leigh-on-Sea, Essex
Tel 0702 72281/714025
Wave Records, 1 Hoxton Square, London N1
Tel 01 729 2476/2440
WEA Records, 20 Broadwick Street, London W1V 2BH
Tel 01 434 3232
Weasel, 10 St Mary's Hill, Stamford, Lincs PE9 2DP
Tel 0780 51736
Web Records, 1 Ash Leicester Road, Nr Loughborough, Leicestershire LE12 8UE Tel 0509 413663/416041
Well Suspect Records, 390 High Street North, London E12
Tel 01 508 5169
West 4 Tapes & Records, 94 Sandy Lane South, Wallington, Surrey
Tel 01 647 1543
WFE Promotions & Management, Tower Cottages, Whaddon Road, Mursley, Milton Keynes Tel 0296 72584
White Lodge Records, P.O. Box 117, London SW12 9HT
Tel 01 675 5584
Why-Fi Records, Warehouse D, Metropolitan Wharf, Wapping Wall, London E1 9SS Tel 01 481 1722
Wilcox Organisation – Zodiac, 1099a Finchley Road, London NW11 Tel 01 455 6620
Vernon Williams Associates, 10 Green Street, London W1
Tel 01 493 4178
Wimp Records, 2 Field Row, Kingston, Cambridgeshire,
Tel 022026 3875
Witch Records, 124 Wheatlands, Heston, Middlesex TW5 0SW
Tel 01 577 1310
Wow It's Now, 34 Frank Street, Bradford 7 Tel 0274 577868
Xcentric Noise Records & Tapes, 17 West End Road, Cottingham, N. Humberside Tel 0482 843411

Yardrose Productions, 38 North Row, London W1
Tel 01 491 3175
Yob Records, 15 Hackworth Street, 4 Rainhill Way, Bow,
London E3 Tel 01 981 4825
Young Blood Records, 6 Heath Close, London W5 Tel 01 991
0993
Y Records, 70a Uxbridge Road, London W12
Tel 01 743 2318/2336
Zap! International Records, The Penthouse, 45 Valley Drive,
Harrogate HG2 0JH/59a Connaught Street, London W2
Tel 0423 501019
Zara Music Records, 63 Trent Road, London SW2
Tel 01 737 1729
Zebra Records, 53 Kensington Gardens Square, London W2 4BA
Tel 01 221 5125
Zella Recording Studios, Walker Hall, Ampton Road, Edgbaston,
Birmingham B15 2UJ Tel 021 455 0645
Zero Records, Central Chambers, Market Square, Wellington,
Telford, Shropshire TF1 1DB Tel 0952 3490
Zomba Productions, Zomba House, 165-167 Willesden High Road,
London NW10 3SG Tel 01 459 8899
Zone to Zone Records, 22 York Street, Stourport, Worcestershire
DY13 9EH Tel 02993 77626
Zulu Records, 61a Bold Street, Liverpool 1 Tel 051 709 7047
ZZT Records, c/o Island Records

APPENDIX 2

MUSIC PUBLISHERS

Acuff-Rose Music, 129 Park Street, London W1Y 3FA
Tel 01 629 0392
Albion Music, 119/121 Freston Road, London W11
Tel 01 243 0011
Alice Music, 9 Cavendish Square, London W1M 0DU
Tel 01 995 1191/0522 38589
Allied Music Company, 75 Tottenham Court Road,
London W1V 9PA Tel 01 636 1174
Ambassador Music, 22 Denmark Street, London WC2
Tel 01 836 5996
APB Music Co, 46A Montagu Square, London W1
Tel 01 723 9269
Aristocrat Music, 9/11 Monmouth Street, London WC2H 9DA
Tel 01 836 4761
D & J Arlon Enterprises, 22 Denmark Street, London WC2H 8NA
Tel 01 836 5996
Attic Music (Publishers), 36 Bloemfontein Road, London W12
Tel 01 743 0427
ATV Music, 19 Upper Brook Street, London W1Y 1PD
Tel 01 409 2211
Aura Music, 1 Kendall Place, London W1H 3AG Tel 01 486 5288
Barriers Music, 29 Biddulph Mansions, Biddulph Road,
London W9 Tel 01 286 0420
Basement Music, 6 Pembridge Road, London W11
Tel 01 221 1522
Bayswater Music, 53 Kensington Gardens Square,
London W2 4BA Tel 01 727 0359
BBJ International, 10/12 Carlisle Street, London W1V 5RF
Tel 01 734 4000

Beanstalk Music, 2 Murray Street, London NW1 9RE
Tel 01 485 1257/431 0864
Beaumont Music, 20/24 Beaumont Road, London W4
Tel 01 995 5432
Bee Bee Music, P.O. Box 472, London SW7 2QB
Tel 01 373 3269
Beggars Banquet Music, 17/19 Alma Road, London SW18
Tel 01 870 9912
Belsize Music, 38 North Row, London W1R 1DH
Tel 01 491 3175
Beth Music, 43 Welbeck Street, London W1 Tel 01 398 5331
Big Ben Music, 18 Lancaster Mews, London W2 3QE
Tel 01 723 4499
Big Note Music Productions, 10 Harley Place, London W1
Tel 01 323 1204/5/6
Black & White Music, 9 Devonport, 23 Southwick Street,
London W2 2QF Tel 01 402 9650/5041
Blue Gum Music, 64 Stirling Court, Marshall Street, London W1
Tel 01 434 1839
Blue Mountain Music, 47B British Grove, London W4 2NL
Tel 01 741 1511
Bocu Music, 1 Wyndham Yard, Wyndham Place,
London W1H 1AR Tel 01 402 7433/4/5
Bourne Music, 34/36 Maddox Street, London W1R 9PD
Tel 01 493 6412
Brampton Music, 4th Floor, 9 Carnaby Street, London W1V 1PG
Tel 01 437 1958
Breaker Music, c/o 6/8 Alie Street, London E1 8DE
Tel 01 481 9917
Brent Black Music Co-op, 383 High Road, London NW10
Tel 01 451 4545
Bright Lights Music, 2 Princes Street, London W1
Tel 01 499 7151/720 3183
Bright Music, 34/36 Maddox Street, London W1R 9PD
Tel 01 408 0288

Bron Organisation, 100 Chalk Farm Road, London NW1 8EH
Tel 01 267 4499
Bruton Music, 19 Upper Brook Street, London W1P 1PD
Tel 01 499 6718
BTW Music, 125 Myddleton Road, Wood Green,
London N22 4NG Tel 01 888 6655
Burlington Music Co, 40 South Audley Street, London W1
Tel 01 499 0067
Cable Music, c/o Amber Music, Soho Wharf, Clink Street,
London SE1 Tel 01 403 0986/0964/2058
Cacophonic Music, 42 Park View Road, London NW10 1AL
Tel 01 450 5987
Campbell Connelly & Co, 37 Soho Square, London W1V 5DG
Tel 01 439 9181
Candle Music, 20 Kildare Gardens, London W2 5LU
Tel 01 221 5521
Cara Music, Regent House, 235/241 Regent Street,
London W1A 2JT Tel 01 493 1610
Carlin Music Corporation, 14 Burlington Street,
London W1X 2LR Tel 01 734 3251
Cats Whiskers Music, 17 Crescent Way, London SE4 1QL
Tel 01 691 7803
Cavalcade Music, 22 Bristol Gardens, London W9
Tel 01 289 7281
CBS Songs, 35 Soho Square, London W1V 5DG Tel 01 439 1845
C & D Music, 22 Denmark Street, London WC2H 8NA
Tel 01 836 5996
Centridge, P.O. Box 137, London N7 0EF Tel 01 272 7501
Cha Cha Music, 63 Gordon Mansions, Torrington Place,
London WC1 Tel 01 636 8173
Champion Music, 23 Powis Gardens, London NW11 8HH
Tel 01 455 2469
Chandos Music, 41 Charing Cross Road, London WC2H 0AR
Tel 01 437 1448/5512

Chappell International Music Publishers, 129 Park Street, London W1Y 3FA Tel 01 629 7600
Charly Publishing, 46/47 Pall Mall, London SW1 5JG Tel 01 732 5647
Cherry Music/Mingles Music, 49 Greek Street, London W1 Tel 01 437 7418
Cherry Red Music, 53 Kensington Gardens Square, London W2 4BA Tel 01 229 8753
Choosy Music Publishing, 8/9 Giltspur Street, London EC1A 9DE Tel 01 236 5940
Chorale Music, 29 Paddington Street, London W1H 3RG Tel 01 486 2362
Chrysalis Music, 12 Stratford Place, London W1N 9AF Tel 01 408 2355
City Records, The Charterhouse, Eltringham Street, London SW18 Tel 01 874 5686
Coeur de Lion International, 82 Adelaide Grove, London W12 Tel 01 743 9412
Collins Music, 38 Kendal Street, London W2 Tel 01 258 3891
Colyer Music, 38 North Row, London W1 Tel 01 499 2014
Compact Composers, Compact House, 31 Riding House Street, London W1P 7PG Tel 01 580 1617
La Composition, 18 Ivor Court, Gloucester Place, London NW1 Tel 01 262 0261
Consortway Music, 42 Priory Avenue, London W4 1TY Tel 01 995 7470
Control Music, 48 Portland Place, London W1N 3DG Tel 01 323 4743
Cornucopia Music, 29 North End Road, Golders Green, London NW11 Tel 01 455 4707
Coverpoint Music, 21 Church Road, London SE19 Tel 01 771 1021
Cow Pie Music, 40 Meadowcroft Road, Palmers Green, London N13 4EA Tel 01 882 6378

Crab Lake Music, 262 Holloway Road, London N7
Tel 01 609 7017/8
Dakota Music, 14A Shouldham Street, London W1
Tel 01 723 1063
Danlou Music, 11 Connaught Place, London W2 2ET
Tel 01 402 9463
Dizzy Heights Music Publishing, 3 Monmouth Place, London W2
Tel 01 727 0527
D N O (Publishing), 6 Holyoake Walk, London N2
Tel 01 883 4137
Dr Snuggles Music, 9 Carnaby Street, London W1V 1PG
Tel 01 437 1958
E & S Music, 20-24 Beaumont Road, London W4 5AP
Tel 01 995 5432
Eaton Music, 8 West Eaton Placc, London SW1 Tel 01 235 9046
E G Music, 63A Kings Road, London SW3 4NT Tel 01 730 2162
EMI Music Publishing, 138/140 Charing Cross Road,
London WC2H 0LD Tel 01 836 6699
Faber Music, 3 Queen Square, London WC1N 3AU
Tel 01 278 6881
Fairplay Music, 26 Danbury Street, London N1 8LE
Tel 01 359 6038
Fast Western, 2 York House, Upper Montagu Street, London W1
Tel 01 723 9559/402 4024
Flashfocus Publishing, Vineyard, Sanctuary Street, London SE1
Tel 01 403 0007
Flash Music, 1 Lower James Street, London W1R 3PN
Tel 01 439 3638
Fresh Air Music, 9 Carnaby Street, London W1V 1PG
Tel 01 437 1958
Funzone Music, 12 Allison Road, London W3 Tel 01 993 3021
Geobell Music, 987 High Road, Finchley, London
Tel 01 446 3218
Giant Music Publishing Co, 9/11 Monmouth Street,
London WC2H 9DA Tel 01 836 4761

Gipsy Music, 55 Ellesmere Road, Chiswick, London W4
Tel 01 736 0321
Glassongs, 79 Wellesley Court, London W9 Tel 01 289 3108
Go! Discs Music, Go! Mansions, 8 Wendell Road, London W12
Tel 01 743 3845/3919
Goldbar Music, Vogue House, 1 Hanover Square, London W1
Tel 01 673 8974
Good Move Music, 27 Spedan Close, Branch Hill, Hampstead, London NW3 Tel 01 435 5302
Handle Music, 1 Derby Street, Mayfair, London W1
Tel 01 493 9637
Harbour Music, 16 Hampstead Gardens, London NW11 7EU
Tel 01 458 3436
Harrisongs, 26 Cadogan Square, London SW1X 0JP,
Tel 01 581 1265
Heath Levy Music Company, 184/186 Regent Street, London W1R 5DF Tel 01 439 7731
Heath Music, 4 Yeomans Row, London SW3 2AH
Tel 01 584 2441
Heathwave Music, 184/186 Regent Street, London W1R 5DF
Tel 01 439 7731
Heaven Music, 114 Southill Park, London NW3 Tel 01 435 0710
Hybrid Music, 14 Neals Yard, London WC2 Tel 01 836 8329
Internote, 249/251 Kensal Road, London W10 5DB
Tel 01 969 9414
Intersong Music, 40 South Audley Street, London W1
Tel 01 499 0067
Island Music, 22 St Peters Square, London W6 9NW
Tel 01 741 1511
Dick James Music, James House, 5 Theobald's Road, London WC1X 8SE Tel 01 242 6886
Jobete Music (UK), 16 Curzon Street, London W1Y 7FF
Tel 01 493 1603
Jungle Music, 24 Gaskin Street, London Tel 01 359 8444/9161

Kassner Associated Publishers, Broadmead House, 21 Panton Street
London SW1Y 4DR Tel 01 839 4672/5
Light Music, 23 Bryanston Court, George Street,
London W1H 7HA Tel 01 402 4810
Lionheart Music, 29 Maddox Street, London W1R 9PF
Tel 01 499 0567
Loose Music, 296 High Road, London W4 1PA Tel 01 995 6225
Louvigny Music Company, 38 Hertford Street, London W1Y 8BA
Tel 01 493 5961
Low Grade Music, 23 Rolls Court Avenue, London SE24
Tel 01 737 4580
Magic Frog Music, 184/6 Regent Street, London W1
Tel 01 439 7731
Magnet Music, Magnet House, 22 York Street, London W1H 4FD
Tel 01 486 8151
Management Agency & Music, 24/25 New Bond Street, London
W1
Tel 01 629 9255
Marand Music, 9 Denmark Street, London WC2 Tel 01 836 6231
Marco Music, P.O. Box 212, London SW1 Tel 01 730 7291
Marquis Music Co, 1 Wyndham Yard, Wyndham Place,
London W1 Tel 01 402 7433/4/5
Martin Coulter Music, Alembic House, 93 Albert Embankment,
London SE1 7TY Tel 01 582 7622
David Martin Music, 42 Portland Place, London W1N 3DG
Tel 01 636 8926
Marylebone Music, P.O. Box 212, London SW1 Tel 01 730 7291
Mautoglade Musi, 22 Denmark Street, London WC2
Tel 01 836 5996/7/2405349
MCA Music, 139 Piccadilly, London W1V 9FH, Tel 01 629 7211
Mcasso Music Publishing, 25 Lexington Street, London W1R 3HQ
Tel 01 437 5175/6363
Medrose, 90 Boston Place, London NW1 Tel 01 724 0814/5
Mercury Music Company, 1-3 Upper James Street,
London W1R 4BP Tel 01 734 8080

Midas, 104 Harley House, Upper Harley Street, London NW1 4PR
Tel 01 935 3987
Million Dollar Music Co, 12 Praed Mews, Paddington,
London W2 1QY Tel 01 402 1261
Minder Music, 22 Bristol Gardens, London W9 Tel 01 289 7281
Misty River Music, 11 Oxford Circus Avenue, Oxford Circus,
London W1 Tel 01 439 2568
Mix Music, 85 Tottenham Lane, London N8 9BE
Tel 01 348 1903/0455
Mousekey Music, 38 North Row, London W1R 1DH
Tel 01 629 1423
MPL Communications, 1 Soho Square, London W1V 6BQ
Tel 01 439 6621
Munnycroft, 59A Connaught Street, London W2 Tel 01 402 1326
Music For Living, 48 Frostic Walk, London E1 5LT
Tel 01 377 1413
Music Publishing Holdings, 38 North Row, London W1
Tel 01 409 1584
Music Sales, 78 Newman Street, London W1P 3LA
Tel 01 636 7777
Nancy Boys Music, 56 Wigmore Street, London W1
Tel 01 486 5745
Negus-Fancey Co, 16 Bedford Gardens, London W8
Tel 01 727 2063/229 4188
Neon Music, 64 Stirling Court, Marshall Street, London W1
Tel 01 434 1839
Neptune Music, 31 Old Burlington Street, London W1
Tel 01 437 2066
New Town Sound, 326 Kensal Road, London W10 5BL
Tel 01 969 6651
Nisbet & Beck Music, 18 Lancaster Mews, London W2 3QE
Tel 01 723 4499
Noon Music, 107 Bell Street, London NW1 6TL Tel 01 988 6695
Trisha O'Keefe Music, 19 Acre Lane, London SW2
Tel 01 274 0164

Olofsong Music, 6 Heath Close, London W5 Tel 01 991 0993
Oops Publishing, 26 Cadogan Square, London SW1X 0JP
Tel 01 581 1265
Openchoice, 9 Carnaby Street, London W1V 1PG Tel 01 437 1958
Orange Publishing, 15 Old Church Street, Chelsea, London SW3
Tel 01 351 3340/2008/5809
Oval Music, 11 Liston Road, London SW4 Tel 01 622 0111
Page One Music, 29 Ruston Mews, London W11 1RB
Tel 01 221 7179/7381
Palace Music Co, 40 South Audley Street, London W1
Tel 01 499 0067
Panache Music, 362 York Road, Wandsworth, London SW18 1SP
Tel 01 870 8522
Papa Music, 3 Chalcot Studios, Berkley Grove, London NW1 8XY
Tcl 01 586 9578
Paper Music, 112 Wardour Street, London W1V 3LD
Tel 01 434 2882
Peterman & Co, 14 New Burlington Street, London W1X 2LR
Tel 01 734 3251
Playbox Music, 101 Chamberlayne Road, London NW10 3NP
Tel 01 960 8466
Point Music, 9 Eccleston Street, London SW1 9LX
Tel 01 730 9777
Prestige Music, 1 Wyndham Yard, Wyndham Place,
London W1H 1AR Tel 01 402 7433
Ramalam Music, 38 North Row, London W1 Tel 01 491 3175
Rat Race Music, 10A Belmont Street, London NW1
Razor Music, 52 Red Lion Street, London WC1 Tel 01 242 9397
RCA Music, 155/157 Oxford Street, London W1 Tel 01 437 2468
Red Bus Music (Int), Red Bus House, 48 Broadley Terrace,
London NW1 Tel 01 258 0324
Ritz Music Company, 8/21 Fitzjohn's Avenue, London NW3 5JY
Tel 01 435 5279
Riva Music, 2 New Kings Road, London SW6 Tel 01 731 4131

Rocket Publishing, 125 Kensington High Street, London W8
Tel 01 937 3815
Rondercrest, 296 High Road, London W4 1PA
Tel 01 995 6225/7536
Rondor Music (London) Ltd, Rondor House, 10A Parsons Green, London SW6 4TW Tel 01 731 4161
Rough Trade Music, 137 Blenheim Crescent, London W11
Tel 01 221 2761
Runaway Music, 38 North Row, London W1 Tel 01 499 2014
Sarm Songs, Osborn House, 9/13 Osborn Street, London E1 6TD
Tel 01 247 1311
Satril Music, Satril House, 444 Finchley Road, London NW2 2HY
Tel 01 435 8063
Scarf Music Publishing, Unit E1, 24 Furze Street, London E3
Tel 01 987 1681
Schauer & May, 67 Belsize Lane, Hampstead, London NW3 5AX
Tel 01 794 8038
Sea Breeze Music, 25 Newman Street, London W1P 3HA
Tel 01 323 1272/5
Sea Dream Music, 236 Sebert Road, London E7 0NP
Tel 01 534 8500
Skratch Music, Southbank House, Black Prince Road, London SE1 7SJ Tel 01 735 8171
Skylark Music, 17 Kingsway, Mortlake, London SW14
Tel 01 876 8509
Southern Music, 8 Denmark Street, London WC2H 8LT
Tel 01 836 4524
Southstrand Music, 1 Lower James Street, London W1R 3PN
Tel 01 439 3638
The Sparta Florida, Music Group, Carlton Tower Place, Sloane Street, London SW1X 9PZ Tel 01 235 0168
Spellbound Music, Southbank House, Black Prince Road, London SE1 7SJ Tel 01 735 8171/587 1545
Spring Songs, 24 Old Burlington Street, London W1
Tel 01 434 2973

Stainer & Bell, 82 High Road, East Finchley, London N2
Tel 01 444 9135
State Music, 26/27 Castlereagh Street, London W1
Tel 01 402 2191
Steinar Music, IBC House, 1/3 Mortimer Street, London W1
Tel 01 637 5277
Stiff Music, 115/123 Bayham Street, London NW1 0AL
Tel 01 485 5622
Stiletto Songs, 122 Holland Park Avenue, London W11 4UA
Tel 01 229 3221
Street Corner Music, 59A Connaught Street, London W2
Tel 01 402 1362
Street Tunes, 45 Barrington Court, Muswell Hill, London N10
Tel 01 883 0775
Summersongs, 17 Gosfield Street, London W1P 7HE
Tel 01 631 5221
Summit Music, 38 North Row, London W1R 1DH
Tel 01 491 3175
Tangent Music, 50 Stroud Green Road, London N4 3EF
Tel 01 263 6403
10 Music, 101-109 Ladbroke Grove, London W11
Tel 01 229 1282
Toast Music, 25 Lexington Street, London W1R 3HQ
Tel 01 437 5175/6363
Tooti Frooti Music Publishing, Soho Wharf, Clink Street,
London SE1 Tel 01 403 4950
Topic Records, 50 Stroud Green Road, London N4 3EF
Tel 01 263 6403
Towerbell, 32/34 Gondar Gardens, London NW6 1HG
Tel 01 431 2770
TRO Essex Music, 85 Gower Street, London WC1E 6HJ
Tel 01 636 7665/6
Virgin Music (Publishers), Virgin Mansions, 95/99 Ladbroke
Grove, London W11 1PG Tel 01 229 1282

Waif Productions, 184/188 Regent Street, London W1R 5DF
Tel 01 439 7731
Warner Bros Music, 17 Berners Street, London W1P 3DD
Tel 01 637 3771
Jeff Wayne Music (Publishing), Oliver House, 8/9 Ivor Place, London NW1 6BY Tel 01 724 2471
Bruce Welch Music, 64 Stirling Court, Marshall Street, London W1 Tel 01 434 1839
Westminster Music, 19/20 Poland Street, London W1V 3DD
Tel 01 734 8121
Whild John Music, 12 Thayer Street, London W1M 5LD,
Tel 01 935 8323
Willpower Music Publishing, 31 D'Arblay Street, London W1V 4LR Tel 01 434 4179
World's End Music, 134 Lots Road, London SW10
Tel 01 351 4333
Zomba Music Publishers, Zomba House, 165/167 Willesden High Road, London NW10 3SG Tel 01 459 8899

APPENDIX 3

MANAGEMENT COMPANIES

Albion Management, 119/121 Freston Road, London W11
Tel 01 243 0011
Allied Artistes Management, 75 Tottenham Court Road, London W1V 9PA Tel 01 636 1174
All Round Productions, 2 West Warwick Place, London SW1
Tel 01 834 3811
Angels Production & Music, 284 Pentonville Road, London N1 9NR Tel 01 837 9992/278 8424
David Apps Agency, 113/117 Wardour Street, London W1V 3TD
Tel 01 439 3032

Artist & Record Promotions, 6 Emerson Street, London SE1
Tel 01 928 9779

The Bacon Empire, Empire House, 271 Royal College Street, Camden Town, London NW1 9LU Tel 01 482 0115

Balfe King, 5a Warwick Street, London W1 Tel 01 437 2777

Boadicea Management, 10 Green Street, London W1
Tel 01 493 4178

Peter Brightman/Peter Chalcroft Management, 28 Leinster Mews, London W2 3EY Tel 01 258 3513

Brill Management, 88b Kings Road, Chelsea, London SW3 4TZ
Tel 01 581 3667

Lois Brisebois Management, 120 Wigmore Street, London W1H 9FD Tel 01 486 5661

Brunskill Management, 169 Queens Gate, London SW7
Tel 01 581 3388

Bullet Management, 90 Boston Place, London NW1
Tel 01 724 0814/5723 1062

Centridge Management, P.O. Box 137, London N7 0EF
Tel 01 272 7501

Peter Charlesworth, 68 Old Brompton Road, London SW7
Tel 01 581 2478/9

Cheval Music, 60 Old Crompton Street, London W1
Tel 01 437 3994

City Records, The Charterhouse, Eltringham Street, London SW18
Tel 01 874 5686

Control Music, 48 Portland Place, London W1N 3DG
Tel 01 323 4743

Stephen Cornwell Representation, 23 Premier House, Waterloo Terrace, London N1 1TG Tel 01 354 1007

Cowbell Agency, 153 George Street, London W1 Tel 01 262 7253

Creative Artistes Management, 9/11 Monmouth Street, London WC2H 9DA Tel 01 836 4761

Harriet Cruickshank, 35 Churton Street, London SW1
Tel 01 828 0046

Damage Control Productions, 25 Newman Street, London W1P 3HA Tel 01 323 1272/5
Dark Blues Management, 30 Stamford Brook Road, London W6 0XH Tel 01 743 3292
Ann Dex Agency, 1A Montagu Mews North, London W1H 1AJ Tel 01 935 0413
Theobald Dickson Productions, Richmond House, Richmond Buildings, Dean Street, London W1 Tel 01 439 6904
D N Organisation, 6 Holyoak Walk, London N2 Tel 01 883 4137
Dolphin Lovers, 40 Denbigh Street, London SW1 Tel 01 828 1978
Don't Panic Productions, 65 Bedford Hill, London SW12 9HA Tel 01 675 5584
Basil Douglas, 8 St George's Terrace, London NW1 8XJ Tel 01 722 7142
Eastern Agency, Belmont House, Steele Road, London NW10 0TR Tel 01 451 1183
EG Management, 63a Kings Road, London SW3 4NT Tel 01 730 2162
Eight Ball Management, 134 Lots Road, London SW10 0RJ Tel 01 351 4333
ESP Music & Management, 4a Newman Passage, London W1 Tel 01 580 7118
European Music Agency, 136 Cromwell Road, London SW7 Tel 01 370 1303
Fatcat Management, 15 Eynham Road, Wood Lane, London W12 Tel 01 743 9912/740 0710
Kate Feast Management, 43A Princess Road, London NW1 8JS Tel 01 586 5502/3/4
The FX Management Company, 60 Metropolitan Wharf, Wapping Wall, London E1 Tel 01 481 2115/2334
Flash Management, 1 Lower James Street, London W1R 3PN Tel 01 439 3638
Foster Shane Management, 16 Noel Road, London W3 Tel 01 992 1986

Gaff Management, 2 New Kings Road, London SW6
Tel 01 731 4131
Gailforce Management, 59 Shaftesbury Avenue, London W1V 7AA
Tel 01 439 8451
Gama Records, 4A Newman Passage, London W1 Tel 01 749 2455
Noel Gay Artists, 24 Denmark Street, London WC2H 8NJ
Tel 01 836 3941
Gems Tour Management, 39 Amesbury Tower, London SW8
Tel 01 622 6465
Ghost Management, 150 Southampton Row, London WC1
Tel 01 278 3331
Goat Bag Records & Music, 7 Nesbit Close, London SE3 0XB
Tel 01 318 7389
Grand Central Enterprises, Roebuck House, Palace Street,
London SW1E 5BA Tel 01 828 3956
Grant-Edwards Management, 5 Wigmore Street, London W1
Tel 01 493 1004
GRG Management, 45 Mount Ash Road, London SE26 6LY
Tel 01 699 5835
Handle Artists Management, 1 Derby Street, Mayfair, London W1
Tel 01 493 9637
Harvestlodge, 33 Felsham Road, London SW15 1AY
Tel 01 789 4169/788 2287
HEC Enterprises, 25 Newman Street, London W1P 3HA
Tel 01 323 1272/5
Heisenberg, 18 Crofton Road, London SE5 8NB Tel 01 703 7677
HHH Concert Agency, 14 Kensington Court, London W8 5DN
Tel 01 937 0850
Hit & Run Music, 59 Shaftesbury Avenue, London W1V 7AA
Tel 01 439 8451
Hobsons Choice, 18 Tennyson Road, London SW19 8SH
Tel 01 540 6768
Hollywood Robots, 38-40 Upper Clapton Road, London E5 8BQ
Tel 01 806 0071/4

Robert A Holmes, Personal Management, 12 Holly Park Gardens, London N3 Tel 01 346 8415
Arthur Howes (London), 8 Bridford Mews, London W1N 1LQ Tel 01 637 7754
Identity Management/Records, 17 Gosfield Street, London W1 Tel 01 631 5221
Inflatable Productions, 84/86 Tottenham Lane, London N8 7EE Tel 01 348 0029/6330
Ingpen & Williams, 14 Kensington Court, London W8 5DN Tel 01 937 5158
Intensive Care Management, 91 North End Road, London NW11 Tel 01 458 5742
International Artistes Representation, 235 Regent Street, London W1 Tel 01 439 8401/5
Susan James Personal Management, 110 Westbourne Grove, London W2 Tel 01 727 8636
Terry King Associates, 9/11 Monmouth Street, London WC2H 9DA Tel 01 836 4761
Tony Lewis Entertainments, 235/241 Regent Street, London W1A 2JT Tel 01 734 2285/6/7
Lewis-Joelle, 108 Frobisher House, Dolphin Square, London SW1V 3LL Tel 01 828 7132
Liaison & Promotion Company, 70 Gloucester Place, London W1 Tel 01 935 5988
Lionheart Music, 29 Maddox Street, London W1R 9PF Tel 01 499 0567
Lip Service Enterprises, 2 Unwin Mansions, Queens Club Gardens, London W14 9TH Tel 01 385 3759
London Artists, 73 Baker Street, London W1M 1AH Tel 01 935 6244
London City Entertainments, 127 Aldergate Street, London EC1A 4JQ Tel 01 253 2276
Robert Luff, 294 Earls Court Road, London SW5 9BB Tel 01 373 7003/1070
Jo Lustig, P.O. Box 472, London SW7 2QB Tel 01 373 3269

Norman McCann, Grand Buildings, Trafalgar Square,
London WC2 5HN Tel 01 930 5240
The Management Co, 351 Edgware Road, London W2 1BN
Tel 01 402 6954
Arthur Martin, Concert Promotions, 8 The Path,
London SW19 3BL Tel 01 540 9648
Mike Malley Entertainments, 10 Holly Park Gardens, London N3
Tel 01 346 4109/4293
Harry Maloney Management, 18/19 Warwick Street, London W1
Tel 01 437 9992/6
Management Agency & Music, 24/25 New Bond Street, London
W1 Tel 01 629 9255
Manic Music, 22/23 D'Arblay Street, London W1V 3FH
Tel 01 434 3035/6
Manna Entertainments & Management, 9 Carnaby Street,
London W1V 1PG Tel 01 437 1958
Marand Music Productions, 9 Denmark Street, London WC2
Tel 01 836 6231
Marathon Records, 30 Great Portland Street, London W1
Tel 01 637 2256/3067
March Music, 2 York House, Upper Montagu Street, London W1
Tel 01 723 9559/402 4024
Marina Martin Management, 7 Windmill Street, London W1
Tel 01 323 1216
Mava Music, P.O. Box 386, London W5 1LS Tel 01 997 7346
Bruce May Music Mng, 11 Oxford Circus Avenue, Oxford Circus,
London W1 Tel 01 439 2568
Maze UK, 65 Duke Street, London W1 Tel 01 409 2399
Millar Bourne Management, 65 Chalton Street, London NW1
Tel 01 387 4451
Mix Management, 85 Tottenham Lane, London N8 9BE
Tel 01 348 1903/0455
Motmot, 84 Arthur Road, London SW19 Tel 01 946 9780
MS Management Services, Warehouse 0, Metropolitan Wharf,
Wapping Wall, London E1 Tel 01 488 4880

Dennis Muirhead Company, 81/83 Walton Street, London SW3 2HP Tel 01 373 8629

Music International, 27A Queens Terrace, London NW8 Tel 01 586 7576

Alec Myles Personal Management, 144 Glenesk Road, London SE9 1RE Tel 01 850 1726

Nada Pulse Music Productions, 10 Southwick Mews, London W2 Tel 01 262 7377

NDS Promotions, 38 Leyland House, Viewfield Road, London SW18 Tel 01 870 0742

Negus-Fancey Co, 16 Bedford Gardens, London W8 Tel 01 727 2063/299 4188

Newjag, 7 Chalcot Road, London NW1 Tel 01 586 3434

Nomis Management, 17 Gosfield Street, London W1P 7HE Tel 01 631 5221

Oak Productions, 10 Stanley Gardens, London W3 Tel 01 743 2362

Oddball Productions, P.O. Box 87, London NW1 8NF Tel 01 485 0625

Outlaw Management, 5A Warwick Street, London W1 Tel 01 437 2777

Owen/Evans Artists Management, 142 Montagu Mansions, London W1H 1LA Tel 01 935 2248

Ozone Management, 12 Allison Road, London W3 Tel 01 993 3021

Larry Page, 29 Ruston Mews, London W11 1RB Tel 01 221 7179/7381

Pan Agency, 10 Sutherland Avenue, London W9 2HQ Tel 01 289 6161

Panda Promotions, 10 Taylor Court, London E15 Tel 01 534 1439

Paradime Music & Management, 22 Faroe Road, London W14 Tel 01 602 3289

Part Rock Management, 1 Haviden House, 71 Baker Street, London W1M 1AH Tel 01 935 2171/0051

Don Percival Artists' Promotion, 38 North Row, London W1
Tel 01 499 0695
Performing Artists Network, 10 Sutherland Avenue,
London W9 2HQ Tel 01 289 6161
Phantom Music, 10 Southampton Row, London WC1
Tel 01 278 3331
Players Management, 99 Montagu Mansions, London W1H 1LF
Tel 01 935 8034
Promotion & Management International (PMI), 25 Duke Street,
London W1 Tel 01 935 9017
PVA Management, 100 Park Street, London W1Y 3RJ
Tel 01 408 0841
Queen Productions, 46 Pembridge Road, London W11
Tel 01 727 5641
Radialchoice, 17 Nelson Road, London SE10 Tel 01 853 5899
R & R Music, Grafton House, 2/3 Golden Square, London W1
Tel 01 439 8442
Razzamatazz Management & Productions, Regent Palace Hotel,
P.O. Box 482, Piccadilly Circus, London W1A 4BZ
Tel 01 439 1452
Roar Enterprises, Queens Studios, 121 Salisbury Road,
London NW6 6RG Tel 01 624 6060
Rock Artistes Management, 2 Unwin Mansions, Queens Club
Gardens, London W14 9TH Tel 01 385 3759
Rosebud Music, 8 Northways College Crescent, London NW3
Tel 01 722 2030
Sea Breeze Productions, 25 Newman Street, London W1P 3HA
Tel 01 323 1272/5
Self Promotions, 86 Winterton House, Deancross Street,
London E1 2QS Tel 01 790 9028
Seventh Sun Productions, 1 Southfield Road, London SW18 1QW
Tel 01 870 5667
John Sherry Management, Queens Theatre, 51 Shaftesbury
Avenue, London W1V 8BA Tel 01 437 0814

Sinister Management, 138 Park Lane, London W1
Tel 01 493 8366
Sky Writing Management, Mews House, 33 Knox Street,
London W1H 1FS Tel 01 723 3271
Solida Leisure & Entertainment Group, 5 Robertson House,
Tooting Grove, London SW17 Tel 01 672 4566
Dorothy Solomon Associated Artistes, 40 Hyde Park Gate,
London SW7 5DT Tel 01 589 4749
Sound Management, Whitehall Theatre, 14 Whitehall,
London SW1 Tel 01 839 3686
Sour Grape, 82 Pathfield Road, London SW16 Tel 01 677 0948
Springtime, Norfolk Mansions, Lithos Road, London NW3
Tel 01 435 1166
SRP, 25 Hayter Road, London SW2 Tel 01 737 1729
Stallion Artists, 76 Roebuck House, Stag Place, London SW1
Tel 01 828 0227
Star-Track International Agency, 120 Wigmore Street,
London W1H 9FD Tel 01 486 5661
Street Tunes, 81 Harley House, Marylebone Road, London NW1
Tel 01 486 1816/0427/2140/5584
Strongman Management, 56 Pembroke Road, London W8
Tel 01 603 0083
Falcon Stuart, 59 Moore Park Road, London SW6 Tel 01 731 0022
Summerton Burton Management, 46 South Molton Street,
London W1Y 1HE Tel 01 493 5737
Sun Artistes, 9 Hillgate Street, London W8 Tel 01 727 2791
Swingbest, 60 Weston Street, London SE1 Tel 01 403 4166
Sylvia Music, 122 Chancery Lane, London WC2 Tel 01 408 0455
Talent Artists, 37 Hill Street, London W1X 8JY Tel 01 493 0343
Talent Incorporated, South Bank House, Black Prince Road,
London SE1 Tel 01 735 8171
Talk Back Management & Productions, 11 Oxford Circus Avenue,
231 Oxford Street, London W1R 1AD Tel 01 439 9322
Target Entertainments, 8/9 Giltspur Street, London EC1A 9DE
Tel 01 236 5940

Textured Images, 38 Mount Pleasant, London WC1
Tel 01 837 8261
Topland Management, 30 Great Portland Street, London W1
Tel 01 637 2256/3067
Towerbell, 32/34 Gondar Gardens, London NW6 1HG
Tel 01 431 2770
Trends Management, 5th Floor, 40/42 Osnaburgh Street,
London NW1 3ND Tel 01 387 3222
Denis Vaughn Management, 7th Floor, Heathcote House,
20 Saville Row, London W1 Tel 01 486 5353
Richard Vernon Management, 9 Thorpe Close, Portobello Green,
London W10 Tel 01 960 7192
Worlds End Management, 134 Lots Road, London SW10
Tel 351 4333
Olav Wyper, 17 Priory Road, London NW6 4NN Tel 01 624 1384
Zomba Management, Zomba House, 165/167 Willesden High
Road, London NW10 2SG Tel 01 459 8899

APPENDIX 4

RECORD PROMOTERS AND PLUGGERS

Al Promotion, 19 Acre Lane, London SW2 Tel 01 274 01674
All Stars Music Company, 46 South Moulton Street,
London W1Y 1HE Tel 01 409 3122
Clive Banks (Modern Media), Suite 1, 20 Broadwick Street,
London W1 Teel 01 734 7638
Bullet, 90 Boston Place, London NW1 Tel 01 724 0814
De Wolfe, 80/88 Wardour Street, London W1 Tel 01 439 8481
Gary Farrow Enterprises, 1 Darby Street, London W1
Tel 01 493 9637

Ferrt Plugging Company, 3 Monmouth Place, Monmouth Road, London W2

Jackie Gill Promotions, 3 Chalcot Studios, Berkley Grove, London NW1 Tel 01 586 9578

Tony Hall Promotions, 4th Floor, 9 Carnaby Street, London W1V 1PG Tel 01 437 1958

Instore Promotions, 10 Barley Mow Passage, London W4 Tel 01 994 6477

RAP (Radio and TV Promotion), 29 Biddulph Mansions, Biddulph Road, London W9 Tel 01 280 0420

Sunshine Plug Company, 3 Monmouth Place, Monmouth Road, London W2 Tel 01 727 1202

Denis Vaughn Record Promotions, 7th Floor, Heathcote House, 20 Saville Row, London W1 Tel 01 486 5353

Waxie Maxie Press & Radio Promotion, 284 Derinton Road, London SW17 Tel 01 672 6918

INDEX

Notes